Publisher's

The response to Paul Madaule's *When Listening Comes Alive* has been gratifying. The first edition sold out in the first year. A Spanish edition is scheduled for release in September 1994 and requests have been received for translation into French, Italian, and Japanese. This is a tribute to the quality of Paul's message and to the efficacy of the Tomatis Method.

While Paul's book takes a broader perspective than the Tomatis Method it is evident that Paul has stirred interest in Dr. Tomatis and his work. Despite the success of Dr. Tomatis' Autobiography and a few other translated works, the English speaking world has never fully understood or utilized the Tomatis Method. The response to *When Listening Comes Alive* indicates that perhaps things are changing. People throughout the world have found Paul's personal story very compelling and they want to know more about Dr. Tomatis and the method which enabled Paul, a dyslexic young Frenchman, to overcome his disability and to write such an articulate book in English!

When Paul first shared his dream of writing a book about his personal and professional experience of the Tomatis Method I strongly encouraged him with the promise that Moulin Publishing would make him its first author and *When Listening Comes Alive* its first book. It was an easy decision since Moulin Publishing was created to publish meaningful messages that might not otherwise make it to market. We at Moulin are pleased *When Listening Comes Alive* made it to market and was so well received. We are proud to release this second edition, with its corrections, enlarged format and lay flat binding. We thank the readers of the first edition who sent us their suggestions for improvement.

Ed Boyce
September 1994

When Listening Comes **Alive**

A Guide to
Effective Learning and
Communication

Paul Madaule

Moulin

CANADIAN CATALOGUING IN PUBLICATION DATA

Madaule, Paul, 1949
When listening comes alive:
    a guide to effective learning and communication

2nd ed.
Includes bibliographical references and index.
ISBN 0-9697079-1-6

1. Listening   2. Communication   I. Title

BF323.L5M3 1994   153.6´8   C94-900766-8

For information contact
Moulin Publishing
P.O. Box #560
Norval, Ontario
L0P 1K0
Canada

Printed in Canada.

To My Parents, Marguerite and Pierre

Acknowledgements

This book would not have reached completion or at least, would not have taken its actual form without the input and help of many colleagues and friends. I wish to say thank you to all of them.

Thank you in particular Mary Jo and Michael Ard, Harl and Jimmy Asaff, Gloria Assmar, Judy Belk, Virginia Chenillo, Wynand Du Plessis, Emilia Flores, Lise Gilmor, Shelley Hainer, Laura Lane, Guillaume Monod, Randall Murphy, Lyn Rasmussen, Barbara Rosenthal, Bob Roy, Roland Viraben, Brad Weeks, Jan Whitford, Tim Wilson and Frances Wood for their comments on the manuscript.

A special thanks to Dusya Broytman for her help editing the first versions of the manuscript. Thank you also to Maya Mavjee and Cara Scime who took the manuscript from where I had left it and made it a book. And Claude Primeau for his sound advice.

This book is a reflection of many years of teamwork. I would like to thank all those who have given their time, expertise and enthusiasm in the making of The Listening Centre. My appreciation goes in particular to Tim Gilmor, co-founder of The Listening Centre. Tim's contribution has been invaluable for the development of the concept of listening and of the Tomatis Method in North America. Thank you Tim for your collaboration and friendship.

MDS Health Group was at the origin of the implementation of the Tomatis Method in North America. From their management team I have learned what professionalism, leadership and teamwork really mean. I am most grateful for their contribution to my work and life in Canada.

Thank you to Ed Boyce for his ongoing support and encouragement throughout the writing of this book. And in giving me the honour of being the first author on the Moulin Publishing list.

I finally want to express my gratitude to Alfred "Tom" Tomatis and his wife Lena for their most precious support and direction in the last twenty-five years. Without them, this book and its content would not be. I hope this book will shed some light on the originality and magnitude of Dr. Tomatis's contribution in the field of Human Sciences.

Contents

Introduction

What great news! Michael is all smiles when he announces that he just graduated from university. He is now a mechanical engineer. It has been nine years since he first came to see me for help. At that time, when he was failing his subjects and his teachers were considering special education, who could have predicted this?

And who would have thought that the frustrated, awkward, angry and difficult youngster would have become the charming, composed and confident young man standing in front of me. His parents are still talking about his rapid and drastic transformation following his "ear tune-up," as they came to call it. For me, Michael is still Michael. It is just that before he could not show his potential — now he can. Before he didn't know how to listen — now he does.

If the idea of a radical transformation such as Michael's is difficult to accept, it is because we usually tend to associate the ear with hearing alone. Yes, we do hear with our ears, but this doesn't mean that hearing is the ear's sole function. The concept of our ears as two microphones sticking out on both sides of our head not only gives a narrow and incomplete idea of what the ear is, but badly distorts our understanding of its role in our life.

A major part of the sensory energy received by the brain comes through the ears. They control balance, body movements and coordination; they permit language; they make us speak eloquently and sing in tune; they even control our eyes when we read and our arm, hand and finger movements when we write. And, as if that were not enough, they also protect us against what we do not want to hear, starting with the sounds of our own body. Interconnected with several different levels of the brain, the ears act as a double antenna receiving messages from both the body and the environment. They are a link between the world within and the world without. Listening — the ability and the desire to use our ears — brings about the harmony both within us and in our relationship with others.

But when listening does not develop well, the harmony is broken, communication is cut off. Problems as diverse as speech and language impairments, hyperactivity, depression, autism, feeling overwhelmed or lacking a direction in life may be some of the results. Reading problems such as dyslexia and other learning disabilities have seldom been looked at and treated as listening problems. Perhaps this is why remedial approaches used to help children with such problems are often so frustratingly ineffective.

Like any other skill, listening can be maximized. Even those who have — or think they have — a normal capacity for listening will benefit from the "Earobic" exercises presented in the book. Enhancing listening skills facilitates assimilation of a foreign language, it allows better appreciation of music, it can even make one sing in tune. Executives comment that better listening significantly enhances their productivity — and leaves them with enough energy to enjoy an evening out after a busy workday. Listening enriches the voice quality, thus facilitating communication; it also increases one's creativity.

When Listening Comes Alive is not the work of a theoretician, an academic or a researcher. It is a personal statement. I suffered from problems quite similar to Michael's until my adolescence. Dr. Alfred Tomatis, a French physician who developed a breakthrough method of sound stimulation, helped me overcome what he diagnosed as a listening problem.

Inspired by the dramatic results, I have spent the last twenty years applying the Tomatis Method and helping people of all ages who have exhibited a wide variety of problems related to listening. These years of work led me to a firm conviction that a lot can be done to improve listening skills at every stage of our life, without the constraints of a clinical environment and specialized equipment. My chief motivation in writing this book is to share my knowledge and experience so that you can benefit from them. I think that having seen firsthand the dramatic difference improved listening makes puts me in the best position to talk about it.

Because of my own history, I give special emphasis to the area of learning disability — a problem that affects more than one-third of school-age children. For parents and teachers, the book provides valuable information and insight on how to prevent and treat such problems.

What is listening? How does it develop? What does it do for us? What are the multiple facets of a listening problem? How can we identify, protect, improve and exercise listening? These are some of the questions raised and answered in this book.

Part I — Listening Unveiled

Listening Unveiled tells the story of how the diagnosis and treatment of my own listening problems led me to become a practitioner of the very method of auditory stimulation which helped me overcome my difficulties. I go on to explain the workings of the Tomatis Method and its numerous applications. The consistent results obtained with this method have led to a re-thinking of the traditional concept of how the ear works and of the various roles it plays in our lives. We will explore this new and rather unorthodox way of viewing the ear and listening.

When Listening Comes Alive

My parents tried everything available in France in the sixties, to understand what was wrong with me and to do something about it. They took me to psychologists, psychiatrists and orthophonists — the French equivalent of a speech therapist. All the specialists agreed that I was bright and that there was nothing wrong with my brain, body, or mind. Then why was I having difficulties at school? I had to repeat three grades and kept getting the lowest marks. The answer of the many specialists was *dyslexia* — a mysterious name that I could never pronounce properly.

Of course, I understood that dyslexia meant difficulty in reading and writing, but then I already knew I had that problem. Some experts went so as far as to describe certain signs of dyslexia, such as reversals of words or letters, or confusions of right and left.

What could be done to overcome this dyslexia? There were as many opinions as there were specialists, and all kinds of therapies and tutoring sessions were recommended. They were all alike to me and they all meant more work after school or during the holidays... with no results.

LOSING GROUND

Year after year, I was losing ground; school was becoming a nightmare. The situation at home had

Year after year, I was losing ground; school was becoming a nightmare. The situation at home had always been tense, but by the time I reached puberty, the conflicts had become unbearable.

always been tense, but by the time I reached puberty, the conflicts had become unbearable. The report cards I brought home were a source of constant arguments between my parents. According to my mother, I was simply lazy. My father was more understanding and always ready to give me another chance. Originally, I would shy away from the arguments and bite my nails in a corner. Then, I started to interject, making matters even worse. This, together with endless disputes between my brother, my sister and myself resulted in yelling, crying, and slammed doors. It was hell for everybody.

When I won a class competition in painting — the first time I ever won anything at school — I started building up great hopes for my artistic talents, and art quickly became my only window into the future. I would spend hours sketching and painting, at the expense of my school work. Modern art seemed to suit me perfectly with its freedom of expression and with what appeared to be its improvisations, with its tolerance for distortion and disharmony. It was only later when I began to study the work and technique of the modern masters — Matisse, Klee, Kandinsky, Picasso — in more depth that I realized that before becoming "modern," they had all followed the path of traditional art and all had traditional educations. School again? The very thought brought me down to earth and the art window started to close — there was nothing I could see myself doing in the future, nothing I felt like doing.

Friends and activities such as scouting had played a very important role in my life, but by the age of sixteen I gave it all up and was spending more and more time alone in my room, just listening to the same songs over and over again.

At the end of the American equivalent of grade nine, when I was seventeen, I had failed all subjects. However, because I was two years older than my classmates, repeating the grade was out of the question. What could I do? Perhaps I could become an apprentice or switch to a vocational school. But I was so clumsy and so poorly coordinated that I couldn't even put the chain back on my bike. I could never remember which way the screwdriver had to be turned; my fingers would tremble with fear at the mere thought of using a hammer. Most of all, I could not picture myself making a living that way. The school finally came up with a solution: I was allowed to audit the grade ten courses without writing the exams. After a few weeks of that, I gave up school altogether.

I now had a lot of time on my hands and I spent some of it in a monastery a bicycle ride away from my hometown. It was an oasis of peace, away from the family tensions and the isolation of my own room. I enjoyed watching the monks doing artwork. One of the monks, Father Marie, was always there to listen to me and to give me friendly encouragement.

One morning, Father Marie unexpectedly arrived on my doorstep. He had just heard a lecture on dyslexia by a physician visiting the monastery. What the doctor described during his lecture was strikingly similar to the problems I had — and not just the problems with school. The physician consented to meet me before going back to Paris that afternoon.

> What could I do? Perhaps I could become an apprentice or switch to a vocational school. But I was so clumsy and so poorly coordinated that I couldn't even put the chain back on my bike. I could never remember which way the screwdriver had to be turned; my fingers would tremble with fear at the mere thought of using a hammer.

A Locomotive Astray in the Meadow

As soon as we arrived in the monastery, I was sent to a room filled with all kinds of electronic machines. I sat down, and a monk explained that he was going to test my ears by using headphones. The instructions were straightforward. I had to raise my hand as soon as I heard a beep — my right hand if I heard it in the right ear, left hand if I heard it in the left one. In the next part I heard many beeps one after another, and I had to say if the sound I was hearing at the moment was higher or lower than the one before. This test was identical to hearing tests I'd previously had, and I could not understand the reason for it as I already knew that my hearing was fine.

The monk handed me the result of my test and sent me to the park of the abbey. There I met the doctor, a completely bald man who stood very straight and introduced himself. "Tomatis" he said, shaking my hand. He then asked me to give him the paper I had in my hand and suggested that we talk while walking along the paths of the park.

After a quick glance at the graphs of the test, he started asking me all kinds of unexpected questions. We talked about everything from family to sexuality and modern art. I was surprised by how much he knew about art and the artists I liked. A doctor who held consultations in the park of an abbey, talking about contemporary art — I could not believe it! I quickly forgot that I was speaking with a doctor and started to chat with a man, an easy-to-talk-to man who took a genuine interest in my views and who understood them even if they were not clearly spelled out. I talked about what preoccupied me at the time: the isolation I felt, my ambivalence about religion, my parents' lack of understanding, the artistic value of The Beatles and Bob Dylan…. Dr. Tomatis had opinions on everything. They often differed from my own, but he always made me feel that my view counted.

In the course of our conversation, Dr. Tomatis described with amazing clarity the world of confusions, contradictions, and conflicts in which I lived and which made my life miserable — my inhibition, temper tantrums, absent-mindedness, the difficult relationship with my parents, fits of anxiety, extreme shyness, sleepless nights, difficulty expressing myself, fear of the future, clumsiness. It was hard to believe that a test of my ears could tell him so much information about me. He also explained that there was nothing abnormal about me and my difficulties were not my fault. They were nobody's fault.

As a conclusion, Dr. Tomatis told me, "You are like a locomotive astray in the meadow. You have to be put back on track." This image summarized what I had gone through for years, and it became my Ariadne's thread for years to come. He then added that if I wanted to get rid of my "annoying little problems," he would be glad to help me at his centre in Paris. Should I decide to come, he asked that I bring with me a recording of my mother's voice.

> As a conclusion, Dr. Tomatis told me, "You are like a locomotive astray in the meadow. You have to be put back on track." This image summarized what I had gone through for years, and it became my Ariadne's thread for years to come.

Alone again, I continued to walk in the park trying to recollect the conversation in its most minute details. I was extremely enthusiastic about what I had heard, and yet the only question I had asked Dr. Tomatis about his treatment was if it would change my dreams and aspirations. That day I realized that it's one thing to want to change, but to actually change is another. Changing means letting some things go. Would I have to relinquish my dreams?

As I continued to recall our conversation, I suddenly realized that he had never brought up school. He had reduced years of difficulties, disappointments and failures to "annoying little problems."

I tried to explain to my parents what the treatment involved. I remembered Father Marie saying that Dr. Tomatis's therapy consisted of listening to sounds modified by special electronic machines. My enthusiasm had more of an impact on them than my explanation.

A few weeks later, in June 1967, I found myself on the platform of the Gare d'Austerlitz in Paris, suitcase in my hand, a tape recording of my mother's voice in my pocket, dreams in my head and hopes in my heart.

THE FIRST PART OF THE SOUND PROGRAM

I was to attend Dr. Tomatis's centre every day for four weeks, and I quickly learned the daily routine. When I arrived in the morning, the receptionist gave me four tickets, one each for a half-hour session. My name and a code made up of letters and numbers were written on each of them.

I would then go to another room where I was greeted by a lady who took my tickets and indicated where I should sit. She would then put headphones on my ears, place a reel on a tape recorder and set the many knobs of an imposing machine with flickering lights, while asking if the volume was comfortable for me. She would then give me paper, crayons, paints and brushes and suggest I spend the time drawing and painting.

I was not alone in the room. Some people slept, others painted, wrote, knitted, talked to each other or with one of the *éducatrices* — the ladies looking after us. There were people in booths, sitting erect on high stools and singing or talking into microphones with our headphones on; we must have all looked like creatures straight out of a science fiction movie.

The noises that I heard through the headphones, scratchy, static noises which were unlike anything I had ever heard before, intensified my feeling of being in a science fiction movie. These sounds, not at all disagreeable, seemed to come from faraway, as if they were from another world. Gradually, I was able to identify some isolated words, then whole sentences would pop out of this sound jumble. It was a few weeks before I realized that it was my mother's voice that I had been listening to all along.

I remember that during those first weeks I had the sensation of living in a muffled environment away from the street noises, and the busyness of Paris. It was as if I were on a cloud.

Once or twice a week I had an interview with Dr. Tomatis. I knew perfectly well by now why I was doing the program, but I needed to hear the reasons again and again. The clarity and richness of his explanations fascinated me.

Before each of my interviews, I had a test similar to the one the monk had given me at the abbey. Dr. Tomatis explained that this test not only indicated whether or not I was hearing properly, but also gave him information on *how* I was hearing. Among other things, my test showed that the language sounds I heard were mixed and distorted, as if they were coming from a poorly tuned radio. That is why I often had to ask people to repeat themselves and frequently heard one word instead of another. Because I was used to perceiving sounds this way, I was not aware of it, just as we forget that we don't see colors as they really are when we wear sunglasses for a long time.

Once the whole class had laughed to the point of tears after I described Plato's myth of the cave (*caverne* in French) as the myth of the tavern (*taverne* in French). I saw Plato's characters sitting around tables, drinking wine and beer in a dark and smokey tavern, shadows of pedestrians walking on the street cast on the back wall. The whole picture was clear in my mind, but a sound confusion put me "off track" creating a misunderstanding. A distorted perception of words, in turn, affected my understanding of the world.

Tomatis often talked about what he called my *dys-lateralité*: "mixed dominance." While I wrote and drew with my right hand, I used my left hand for virtually everything else. I even had the brakes inverted on the handlebar of my bicycle so that I could reach the rear brake with my left hand. I wore my watch on my right arm because it was easier to put on that way. I never knew which way the key had to be turned to open or close the door. Was the hot water tap on the right or on the left? If the switch was up, was the light on or off?

I learned that the mixed dominance also affected my eyes and ears. In looking at something, I used the left eye to focus. When listening, I tuned into the sounds predominantly with my left ear and I talked "left." This meant that I was using my left ear to control my speech. How did Dr. Tomatis know all that? Apparently, he could see my lips projecting words to the left side of my mouth, and the left side of my face was more animated when I talked. I learned that the route from the left ear to the "language centre of the brain" is longer and therefore less efficient. That explained the time-lapse that occurred when expressing my thoughts in words. The words tried to "catch up" with my ideas and most of the time they arrived too late. This time-lapse caused the stammering, the hesitations, and the difficulties I had in finding the right word. It also accounted for my tendency to substitute one word for another and the fact that I frequently lost my train of thought and shifted from one idea to another in mid-sentence.

> My brain was working faster than my tongue, and I felt it most when in a group discussion. By the time I was finally able to express my ideas, the other people would already be talking about something else.

My brain was working faster than my tongue, and I felt it most when in a group discussion. By the time I was finally able to express my ideas, the other people would already be talking about something else. Another effect of the left ear control was my monotonous and mumbled voice. No wonder nobody in a group had the patience to pay attention to what I had to say!

I also found out that in addition to registering sounds and monitoring speech, the ears control balance and body movements. When, as in my case, the ears did not work in harmony, this control was imprecise and unstable. I understood the reason for my clumsiness, the hard time I had had learning to ride a bike, my dislike of all sports, and my strange duck-like gait, which was the source of many jokes. I also understood why I had to give up guitar lessons: I was unable to dissociate the movements of the right and left hand.

Poor mastery of the body also distorted my perceptions of time and space. It was difficult for me to learn to tell time, and I would wear a watch just for show. It also explained why I had to make the sign of the cross to determine which side was right or left.

My poorly defined notion of time and space also accounted for my lack of organization, which was why my mind was so confused. I was unable to express my ideas in a clear, concise and structured way. When writing, I would get lost in my sentences. Teachers' comments on my essays were always, "good ideas, but poorly worded." I also had a very hard time with syntax. The "floating space" in which I lived was also a reason for my total incompetence in math.

In order to read and write well, one needs not only good control of language, but also good control of the body, and both of these systems are regulated by the ear. The movements of the eyes that are essential to reading, and those of the arms, hands and fingers involved in writing are controlled by the body. In my case, sound analysis and body control were "off," causing all sorts of "annoying little problems" usually described as dyslexia.

Dr. Tomatis added: "the way your ears work, you can't help but think about something else or look out the window after five or ten minutes in the classroom.

It takes too much out of you to listen. Our intelligence should be used to make us smart, but you are using yours to compensate for the distortions."

The purpose of the sound training program was to suppress the distortions that prevented me from clearly perceiving and emitting certain sounds. It was also designed to establish dominance of the right ear. The tuning system of my ear had to be improved — tuning to the language sounds, tuning to the body, tuning to space and time. The sensation of dizziness I had complained of at the beginning of the program was an indication that both my ears were listening and thereby finding a new balance.

Dr. Tomatis also explained that in order to understand the root of my problem one has to go back to the time in life when the ears first started to operate, to the time before birth and during infancy.

The recorded mother's voice modified by electronic filters helps to imitate the way the fetus hears before birth. The use of this voice at the beginning of the sound program allows one to re-experience all the stages of development of the ear and of the desire to communicate.

During one of the interviews, Dr. Tomatis recommended that I spend a month in England instead of going back home. "At the very least you will learn some English, which may be of help to you later."

Discoveries

I was not at all enthusiastic about going to England. Twice before I had spent a month there to improve my English. Both times the family with whom I lived initially tried their best to establish some rapport with me, but no matter how hard I tried I was unable to break the linguistic barrier. They quickly gave up trying and so did I. These trips had done nothing to improve my skills in English, which was one of my weakest subjects.

On the ferry to England, I met a happy-go-lucky French guy. We immediately hit it off. Together we began to "discover" London. We went to Picadilly Circus, Soho, the clubs.... We bought eccentric clothes at Carnaby Street and soon became part of the peculiar world which was London in the late sixties. Despite my serious limitations with English, I could make myself understood, laugh and even make others laugh.

> Despite my serious limitations with English, I could make myself understood, laugh and even make others laugh.

Once I returned to Paris, I began to wonder about what had happened in England. Why had it been so easy to get along with this guy, to have such an instant friendship and all the encounters, the laughter, the fun...? Everything had seemed surprisingly easy, even the English language! I was both puzzled and ecstatic and so excited about the prospect of talking to Dr. Tomatis at my next interview.

When I met with him, he listened to me and then suggested: "Well, after the good time, it's the time to think about serious matters. What plans do you have in mind?" I had none. I had been out of the classroom for more than a year and had forgotten all about schooling. But it was August and classes were starting in September. As I had no ideas, Dr. Tomatis suggested that I enroll at a boarding school close to Paris. The very idea of school made me nauseous, but a boarding school was even worse! I had no choice but to agree. Right there, on the spot, Dr. Tomatis called the headmaster and asked him if there was any room for me in grade eleven.

Once he had hung up the phone, I reminded Dr. Tomatis that I had never gone to grade ten and that I had been the worst student in the class for all the other grades. He told me that he was aware of that but I could not afford to waste any more time. What counted was to get my baccalaureate within two years, and he added: "If you put as much energy into studying as you did into having fun in England, you are sure to succeed."

The Second Part of the Sound Program

Now it was my turn to sit erect on a stool in a small booth. I had to breathe deeply and repeat into the microphone what I heard through the headphones. At the beginning of the sessions, I vocalized to the sound of a Gregorian chant. Then came lists of words and sentences loaded with sounds such as s, ch, f, z. Modified by the electronic filters, these words seemed to whistle in the ears. I also heard my voice whistle when I repeated them. This was an unusual sensation, since I was used to hearing my voice sound very low. Not only did I have to sit straight as a ramrod, but I also had to push my lips forward, as if I wanted to "kiss the microphone," as the recording instructed me. Between sessions, I could rest, listening to scratchy classical music.

Later, I was asked to read out loud, still using the microphone. These reading sessions were tiring and frustrating at first. I would mix up words and hesitate. My voice quickly lost its volume and I would start mumbling. I also found I could not keep up the straight posture for more than a few minutes. An *éducatrice* would come in to remind me of the correct posture and to help me with articulation. She would insist that it was the sound of the words that was important at this stage, not the meaning.

> I remember that during one of these walks I was looking at books in a store and suddenly realized that I was not simply leafing through to look at pictures but was actually reading, and I understood what I read!

Little by little, my voice was becoming stronger, more colourful, more expressive, and the text began to have some meaning. The exercise became more interesting, less tiring. I even started to like it! After these reading sessions, I felt refreshed, invigorated and ready for long walks on the streets of Paris.

I remember that during one of these walks I was looking at books in a store and suddenly realized that I was not simply leafing through to look at pictures but was actually reading, and I understood what I read! Towards the end of August, I could easily read out loud for a full half-hour at the centre. This exercise filled me with physical energy. It was a new sensation, a sort of euphoria. I felt my entire body vibrating. I could go on and on reading aloud, well after the half-hour session was over.

BOARDING SCHOOL

Boarding school was not so bad after all! It wasn't long before I made a few good friends, and I found the teachers quite likeable. Work was hard, but I quickly realized that the sense of not being able to apply the new knowledge in a more general context — the sense of being lost — had disappeared. I was far from being a good student, but I was plugging along. Apart from math, which was still a nut to be cracked, "difficult" no longer meant "impossible."

Throughout the two years of boarding school, I practiced the reading aloud exercise recommended by Dr. Tomatis every day. I would use it to review the French literature texts. More and more often, I found myself reading a book in my spare time. I could now be carried away by a good story.

I spent a lot of my time writing letters to family and friends. "Chatting" on paper was a new and fascinating experience, and for some time my drawing and painting retreated into the background. I started to write poetry; my observations, thoughts and feelings would take the form of free verse. The words replaced paints and brushes to create images. As for lines, there were straight words, curved words, words which would zigzag. As for colours, there were both "hot" and "cold" words. Words could convey light, clarity, shades, darkness or transparency.

On Saturdays, I would take the bus to Paris to continue my program at the centre. From time to time I met Dr. Tomatis, who monitored my progress and gave me advice and encouragement. During the first year in boarding school, I passed my driver's test — the first test I ever passed in my life!

In the French academic system, the baccalaureate is the examination students take at the end of high school in order to get into university. To all of us it was the armoured door between school and freedom.

At first, I didn't believe I could pass the first time around. There were so many horror stories of good students failing after several attempts. On the other hand, there were also few miracle stories of bad students who managed to pass, and those stories were quite contagious. Dr. Tomatis was firm in his opinion: "you can succeed, if your books become your only friends for a while."

> I saw in Dr. Tomatis's technique a concrete, efficient, holistic and humanistic approach that could be used on a large scale. That is what helping people meant to me. It was a therapy of the future.

I turned twenty in February of 1969. Twenty and still at school! It was so humiliating that on my weekend outings in Paris I passed myself off as a university student. It was time I decided to start studying for real, and it worked!

WHAT'S NEXT?

When I told the wonderful news to Dr. Tomatis, he asked about my plans. This time I was prepared for his question. I had already put a lot of thought into it. Helping people always interested me. In the boarding school, I had the opportunity to observe the effect of his sound treatment not only on myself but also on other students. I also heard extraordinary stories from clients I met at the centre. The field of application of this treatment seemed to spread well beyond the language and learning difficulties of children and adolescents. At the centre, there were people of all ages from all walks of life — singers, disabled people, famous actors, expectant mothers, the elderly, religious people. Each and every one of them seemed to benefit from Dr. Tomatis's technique in one way or another. I saw in this technique a concrete, efficient, holistic and humanistic approach that could be used on a large scale. That is what helping people meant to me. It was a therapy of the future.

Several times during my interviews with Dr. Tomatis I had alluded to my wish to study and work with him. His answer invariably had been: "Get your baccalaureate first, then we'll talk."

Now that I had my "bac," I told Dr. Tomatis that I intended to study psychology, and that I would like to be introduced to his work while studying at university. He offered me the position of part-time trainee at the centre and concluded, "Now the real work begins." This was more than twenty years ago, and the work still goes on....

Making Listening **2** Come Alive

Sandy, a bright, attractive ten-year-old, has come to see me about a learning problem. Seated on a swivel stool across from me and next to her parents, she is fidgeting as she answers my questions about her interests, her friends and what she wants to do when she grows up. I am listening for her answers, but I am also watching Sandy on that stool. It is not what she is saying that is of interest, but how she's saying it. I note which questions make her yawn, which ones she asks to be repeated or says she doesn't understand, which she asks Mom or Dad to answer for her. Most importantly, how she uses her body when she is trying to communicate.

The stool on which I have casually directed Sandy to sit rotates easily, letting her turn her body in whichever direction she wishes. She may turn all the way around, stop and face the wall, turn her back to me or her parents. She may lose her posture altogether as if some questions are deflating her, or she may instantly straighten up at others. Although I know she has a natural ability for athletics, the frequent involuntary and uncoordinated movements of her limbs while listening and talking make her appear to have little control of her body.

As this is going on, I am also listening for variations in Sandy's voice quality, rate and intonation. Sometimes she may soften almost to a whisper, then suddenly speak up. She will mumble and have to search painfully for each word and then race off breathlessly. While she talks, I note the side of the mouth from which her speech flows, which side of her face is more animated, which hand tends to move more. I also observe which ear she uses to listen, to "lean into" a conversation. Sandy is right-handed, but she "leads" with her left ear when she listens, and with the left side of her lips and face when she talks. This is a good indicator of a mixed lateral dominance problem.

Sandy's struggle with reading and writing is what brought her to the centre. There is also a clear lack of harmony between what she is saying and how she is using her body to say it. I conclude she is an excellent candidate for the Tomatis Method.

• • •

The Tomatis Method has come a long way since the early 1950s when Dr. Tomatis first started helping opera singers regain their voice by retraining their ear. From helping opera singers to sing again, to bringing an autistic child out of his secret world, the evolution of the Method has been driven by the surprising and often unexpected results of stimulating the ear with sounds. The possible explanation of why it works came later. Out of respect for this chronology of events, I will describe the Method first and explain why it works later. So, if some things in this chapter seem puzzling, bear with me in good faith, and you will find the missing pieces of the puzzle in the following chapters. I can best define the Tomatis Method as a program of sound stimulation and counselling to develop and improve listening.

The Method is still being applied by Dr. Tomatis at his centre in Paris. I have practiced the Method at The Listening Centre in Toronto since 1978, and I also helped set up various centres throughout the United States, Mexico and Panama (see Appendix A for a complete list of the North American centres). All in all, there are almost 200 clinics using the Tomatis Method worldwide.

The sounds used in the Method are designed to reproduce the main stages of development from the point of view of the ear, starting well before birth and continuing until the time we learn to read and write. This sound stimulation program begins with a passive phase in which the ear is trained by means of filtered sounds, and then progresses to an active phase of voice exercises. Throughout the program, counselling provides the support necessary for the client.

> I can best define the Tomatis Method as a program of sound stimulation and counselling to develop and improve listening.

The sequence of listening and language development basically doesn't vary, so the stages of the program are the same for everyone. Only the length and content of each stage changes according to individual needs. An initial assessment similar to Sandy's is always the very first step of the program.

THE INITIAL ASSESSMENT

The goal of the assessment is to determine whether the Tomatis Method can actually be of help, and if so, to tailor the program to each client. The information gathered helps answer three major questions: What could be the causes of the listening problem? What is the nature of the problem itself? How does this problem affect communication with oneself and others?

Reading Sandy's case history, filled out by her parents, I looked for clues as to the first of these questions — where could the problem have originated? I was interested in the details of her early life such as her mother's health and well-being during pregnancy, the circumstances surrounding birth, what her infancy was like, the development of her motor, auditory, visual and language functions. The history of the family is another source of valuable information. How did her parents get along? What happened with the arrival of her baby brother? Or when the family moved to another house? Or when trouble started at school? Or when Sandy was sick? How many ear infections has she had? When? How severe were they?

The centerpiece of the assessment is the Listening Test. Among other things, it helps to answer the second question on the nature of the problem. Sandy's overall listening potential, how she relates to others and the way she sees herself are all reflected in her test. It also gives information about Sandy's body functions such as her balance and posture. From the test, I could tell why she had insisted her parents buy her a guitar — her musical capability was evident, as well as the hard time she had at school. Sandy's desire to listen and when this desire might have been impeded showed in the test as well. The test also gives an idea of one's speech and language skills, as well as the level of energy and creativity.

I encouraged both Sandy's parents to be present for the initial interview, which helps answer the third question — how the problem affects the way Sandy relates to herself and to others. I observe how she communicates and how the whole family interacts during the interview. Seeing Sandy and her family, together with case history, test results and other documents permits me to determine if the sound stimulation program may be of help. When I recommend it, I explain how and to what extent it can help. I make sure to answer any questions Sandy and her parents have.

For adults and most adolescents, the parents don't have to be there for the interview. As with children, I am more interested in the way the information is conveyed than in the information itself. Once I recommend a program, we clearly establish what it is we want to accomplish, and I stress the importance of a commitment on the part of the client. This is particularly true for adolescents who come to see us at their parents' request. I often postpone beginning the program to give youngsters all the time they need to make up their mind. There may be a few more meetings until they decide they are ready to start. Most often it's not the intervention itself they are opposed to, but their parents' opinion and decision about it. The time it takes to allow the adolescents to make up their mind is in no way wasted, and an overwhelming majority do decide to go ahead. In my case, I met Dr. Tomatis without my parents present, and he ingeniously enlisted me in the task of convincing them to let me go ahead. This, I learned, was an ideal way to involve a youngster and it remains an invaluable lesson to me as a clinician.

Not everyone who comes to the centre for an initial assessment will require a listening training program. Sometimes, the program does not apply to the presented problems and I recommend an alternative method. At times all that is needed is some advice on how to create an environment conducive to better listening, how to stimulate and protect it in our everyday lives. You will find the most useful of these suggestions in Part II of this book. I also often recommend an exercise routine that can be done at home without any specialized equipment — the Earobic exercises of Part III.

However, when the program is recommended, I specify its length during the interview. It varies according to the nature and the severity of the problem and the age of the client. An average program is sixty to ninety hours of sound stimulation, and we usually break it down into two fifteen day intensive sessions of about two hours a day. A break of four to six weeks separates the two intensive sessions. Sometimes, a couple of hours a day, only two or three times a week will suffice. However, an intensive beginning is always recommended, as the results are then more dramatic and appear much faster.

THE PASSIVE PHASE

During the first part of the program — the passive phase — Sandy will listen through headphones to sounds modified by Tomatis's ear training device, the Electronic Ear[1]. The chief objective of the passive phase is to recreate the prenatal environment by means of sounds rich in high frequencies; to give Sandy the desire and the energy to use her listening to communicate; and to deal with the forthcoming changes. It also sets the stage for the next phase of the program, the exercise phase.

We call this first part "passive" because Sandy — and other clients — don't have to consciously pay attention to the sounds coming through the headphones or do any voice exercises: they can draw, paint, play, talk, even sleep. In fact, paying attention would impose the "old," distorted listening patterns that we are trying to correct.

The sound stimulation during the passive phase is usually a combination of mother's recorded voice and music by Mozart. The mother's voice is used for children and adolescents, seldom for adults. When, for some reason, it is not available, music alone can produce the desired results.

The recording of the mother reading aloud is modified by means of electronic filters to accentuate the high frequencies in the voice. In fact, the end result hardly resemble the voice; the high squeaky whistling noises are more like sounds from another world — and in a way, they are! Filtered like this, the mother's voice takes the listener back to the womb, building a bridge between that world and the one after birth. It is like a return to the very roots of the listening ear.

The passive phase ends with the so-called sonic birth, which is a progressive defiltering of the voice that reproduces the passage between the prenatal mode of listening and the one that comes after birth. The same method is done with the music of Mozart.

Children's reactions to their mother's voice can be extraordinary to watch, especially for the parents. The children become more affectionate. Those who tended to be distant take to their mother's lap, and start kissing, hugging and embracing her. What a delight for a mother of an autistic child! The "hyper" ones may become still more hyper for a few days, and then calm down, showing more control. The calm and too well behaved ones may start doing unexpected things such as teasing their siblings, becoming noisier, or seeking their mother's attention by acting childishly and using baby talk. They may even become aggressive and antagonistic. And all these children start to listen and speak a lot more.

As I point out to parents during the counselling interviews when their child starts to express his feeling and opinions, what he does *not* like and what he does *not* want are the first to come out. When a well is opened, it is the mud that pours out first, and only then the water. If the child is not given room for these antagonistic reactions, the well may close again. In any event, such negative reactions seldom last for more than a couple of weeks.

At this stage of his program, Shawn, an energetic thirteen-year-old, started to be more curious about things, people and events. He started asking lots of questions. His parents had to be ready, open and receptive. More observant than he had ever been, Shawn would describe a movie he saw or a baseball game he played with an unexpected flurry of details. Where he used to complain that he had no friends, he was now bringing people home. His teacher commented that his hand was always up to answer questions. For me, as well as Shawn's parents, this outburst of enthusiasm, triggered by the filtered sounds, indicated his desire to open up. Shawn was now ready to go on to the next phase of the program.

Adults react to filtered music in their own way. Those who are tense and uptight and have a hard time slowing down say that at first the music makes them feel tired and empty. Then they notice how much calmer they feel; their sleep is so much deeper and more restful! On the other hand, people who tend to be depressed and tired say the music makes them fidgety, upset or angry for the first few days. They have sudden fits of crying or outbreaks of laughter. As time goes on, they feel more and more on top of things, in charge of their life and their emotions. The old overwhelming problems become more manageable or simply disappear. Those who do not sleep well at the outset of the program are surprised to feel more awake in the morning. After a few weeks they are sleeping, on average, two to three hours less each night and feeling better than ever. By the end of the day, they are amazed to realize how much they have accomplished without even giving it a thought.

After complaining of tension and backache, many have physical sensations of well-being throughout their entire body. Clients say that they feel like going for walks, jogging or going back on an exercise program. Some suddenly decide to stop smoking or switch to a healthy diet — and they follow up on it! A project that has been put aside for a long time is now taken up again.

THE ACTIVE PHASE

The second phase is called "active" because it involves exercises. Clients use their own voice to "feed" their ear and stimulate their listening, which in turn controls voice production. During the passive phase, listening is "awakened." Now it is time to apply it to the voice by means of exercises. The clients hear recorded sounds through the headphones and repeat them into a microphone. Both the original sounds and the voice are modified by the Electronic Ear to reproduce accurate listening, and are fed back to the ear through the headphones.

In the active phase, voice production is addressed first with singing and chanting exercises, then speech is introduced through word and sentence repetition, and a reading aloud exercise introduces written language. Each active session lasts half an hour and is followed by another half hour of listening to filtered music or Gregorian chants. This allows the clients to rest and relax between the exercises, while still stimulating the ear.

Younger children sing along with nursery rhyme recordings, whereas older clients vocalize to Gregorian chants. The Listening Therapist is with the clients every step of the way, instructing them on body posture, respiration and production of sounds. Some of the chanting exercises are done with the mouth closed. This humming produces "bone-conducted" sounds, which are extremely dense in the high frequency range, and thereby highly energizing.

The next step of the active phase consists of repetitions of words and sentences rich in "whistling" language sounds, such as s, f, ch, and j. These are high frequency sounds. To give even more "weight" to the exercise in that high-frequency range, the low frequencies of the

> The second phase is called "active" because it involves exercises. Clients use their own voice to "feed" their ear and stimulate their listening, which in turn controls voice production.

sound stimulation are progressively filtered out. The body posture, respiration and sound production techniques learned during the chanting exercises still apply, and the sounds are clearly articulated with the lips projected forward.

By this stage of the program, clients have already realized how much faster, less tiring and how much more fun reading is. Shawn's parents observe that guessing the names on the road signs has become his favorite new game in the car. Furthermore, they often find Shawn with a toy's instruction manual or a magazine in his hands. Now that his voice is strong, rich and well articulated, now that his speech is clear and expressive, all that needs to be done is to add the "eyes" to the "ear-language mechanism." This will bring him to the written language stage of the program.

At this point, clients are asked to read out loud from a book of their choice, while their voice is monitored by the Electronic Ear. As the emphasis during the exercise is on voice quality, they have to read relatively slowly and with good expression. Adults who think reading has never been a problem realize during these sessions that they still have a long way to go to qualify as good readers. After a few tiring, frustrating sessions — particularly for those with a history of reading problems — things become smoother. Little by little, the eyes are being "guided" by the ears, just as the sound of the music literally directs a violinist's fingers. Reading becomes effortless and interesting, as if the text is being read for you, not by you. During my own program, I was so carried away by the reading sessions that I did not feel like stopping. I have seen the same happen to others time and time again.

Reading is usually the first skill to improve during the active phase. Teachers have better things to say about the student's achievement, marks go up. Handwriting gets better and spotting and correcting spelling mistakes seems easier. In fact, mistakes that might not even have been noticed before now stand out. I often hear children complain of making *more* mistakes after starting the program, while their marks on spelling tests get better and better. To sing in tune, you have to be able to hear yourself singing out of tune and thus know what has to be corrected; to spell correctly, you have to recognize where the mistakes are.

Better listening and language functions have profound ramifications for the way one thinks and experiences life. During and after the active phase, I often hear expressions such as "I've got things under control now," "it's all coming together," "I know what I want," or "I know which direction to take." Communication and harmony with others and with life start within ourselves. And a key to this harmony is the link between the ear and voice.

> Reading is usually the first skill to improve during the active phase. Teachers have better things to say about the student's achievement, marks go up. Handwriting gets better and spotting and correcting spelling mistakes seems easier.

At the completion of the program, we recommend daily reading aloud as the main follow-up exercise. This reinforces the newly acquired listening skills, helps maintain a good quality voice and prevents slipping back into old habits. The newly established listening patterns are still fragile; they need time and reinforcement. Reading out loud practiced regularly ensures that the effects of the program are maintained, and that progress continues for the months and years to come.

The Counselling

The interviews I had with Dr. Tomatis during my program were of considerable importance. I needed someone who understood what I was going through and who could explain it to me, someone who could see my potential and talk to me about it, someone who would sound the alarm when I was drifting away, someone to remind me over and over again of the direction I had chosen.

The physicists say that all movement produces heat. This rule applies equally well to human changes. There is no change without tension, without fear and resistance. That is why wanting and actually experiencing a change are two quite different things. If we are living what we feel is a terrible life, with no hope for the future and no ability to communicate, one possible refuge is in dreams and fantasy. But the moment the better world we've been dreaming about arrives, what is there left to dream about? And so, paradoxically, the first question when considering therapy, that comes to mind, may be: "What am I losing?" Losing my dreams was the first fear I expressed when I met Dr. Tomatis. Going from dreaming about a life to actually living it is not that simple. To help deal with the necessary "heat" produced by change, counselling is an integral part of the sound stimulation program. At times, the counselling may take forms other than individual interviews; it may be carried out in a group situation such as workshops. However it is never completely left out.

We normally schedule a counselling interview after every fifteen to twenty hours of sound stimulation. This gives me an opportunity to review changes at a particular stage of the program and, when necessary, to give explanations, advice and recommendations. A listening test taken before each interview provides a graphic illustration of the progress.

> During the interview I am the child's spokesperson and advocate. I use adult language to explain to parents the child's point of view, his beliefs and reactions, his behaviour, his fears and dreams, his needs.

For children, I prefer both parents to be present for the interviews. The parents and I work as a team to help the child to go through the changes, to promote better communication at home and to look ahead. The home is the child's first social nucleus. Open dialogue and understanding at home automatically reflect on all the other social groups that are part of a child's life, namely school, sports teams, their peer group, camp, etc.

During the interview I am the child's spokesperson and advocate. I use adult language to explain to parents the child's point of view, his beliefs and reactions, his behaviour, his fears and dreams, his needs.

My job as an advocate for the child is also to help the parents perceive the child's potential — not his difficulties — and to show them how to reinforce it. Some children misbehave in an attempt to become the centre of attention. The silly and petty things they do are their way of telling others: "I am here, take notice of me!" They are like actors looking for a role, a social *raison d'être*. The solution lies in forgetting the past and giving the child a responsible role. I have seen so many of those "socially difficult" youngsters do excellent work helping younger or handicapped children. This responsibility gives them an identity, a solid foundation. Playing the fool is no longer necessary.

Parents of children with difficulties have very good reasons to be anxious, tense, depressed, disoriented, tired or fed up. What they need is to relax. They need that extra energy which has been missing. They need more than just encouraging words. The help we offer to the parents goes beyond counselling. As part of their child's program, parents listen to music and chant through the Electronic Ear. This relaxes and stimulates them. Counselling shows them what their child needs from them, and the actual sound stimulation gives them the energy necessary to do it.

The sound stimulation program with the Tomatis Method is a relatively short intervention: it has a beginning and a foreseeable end. It is a passage that allows people to establish listening patterns in their quest for growth and independence. The training does not provide anything that was not within a person to begin with — it is not a miracle. Instead, it frees up the hidden resources, the enormous potential.

Who Can Benefit from the Tomatis Method

People of all ages come to us seeking help for a wide variety of reasons. Programs of sound stimulation have been developed to help pregnant mothers relax and better enjoy their experience, while at the same time enriching their voice to enhance the "dialogue" with the unborn child. Reduced time of delivery and a decrease in the number of caesarean sections was noted for mothers who participated in the Tomatis Method.[2] And if you think that isn't early enough, how about starting even before conception; young couples at The Listening Centre remark that the sensory "attuning" helps them to have a more harmonious relationship.

> Often, when I suggest to someone that he may have a listening problem, the person replies that, on the contrary, his ear is too sensitive. "I hear too much," he may say.

Some hospitals in Europe introduce the mother's voice that has been filtered into incubators for premature children by means of small loud speakers. This helps the newborn to compensate for the separation from the mother and for the sensory and emotional prenatal experience that was interrupted.

Children with motor development problems and poor muscle tone, caused by neurological impairments such as cerebral palsy, or a genetic abnormality such as Down's syndrome, can also greatly benefit from the auditory stimulation. These children can start the program as soon as they are able to wear headphones, at eighteen to twenty-four months of age. I hope future technology will allow us to start even earlier.

Children with various language impediments are generally good candidates for the Method. These can be problems with voice production and speech, such as stuttering, or more specific language-oriented difficulties, such as poor or inadequate vocabulary and sentence structure.

Often, when I suggest to someone that he may have a listening problem, the person replies that, on the contrary, his ear is too sensitive. "I hear too much," he may say. And they go on with a long list of examples, such as waking up at the slightest noise or being easily disturbed by background sounds. But, I insist, hearing too much means not listening enough. At its extreme, this is precisely what happens with many autistic children, those who cover their ears with their hands to block a sound, who seem hurt by some noises and afraid of them.[3] For Tomatis, autism is the purest form of "non-listening."[4] In those cases, the listening training program becomes a very powerful tool for help. And it can also come to the rescue when speech and language are not used to communicate with others or absent altogether, as in many cases of autism.

The effectiveness of the sound stimulation has also been illustrated with highly anxious South African primary school children[5] and severely mentally retarded institutionalized children[6].

The sound stimulation program will also be of help to most students who suffer from a learning disability. This includes attentional deficit disorders, poor concentration, hyperactive tendencies, poor organizational skills, difficulty with reading, writing and spelling, as well as some difficulty with math and memory problems. The earliest is always the best time to help, but there is no age limit for positive results with learning disabled people.

A history of hardships at school means a history of failures, of feeling odd and inadequate. Because school is the centre of the child's world, this feeling becomes central in his whole life. The school problems become social and existential ones. Poor self-confidence and self-esteem, negative attitude toward family and friends or withdrawal will be some of the possible side effects. This shift from being just a school problem to one of general maladjustment can start in the early grades. It usually tends to change and by puberty or adolescence can be seen by others as a personality disorder. With these youngsters, counselling becomes an essential part of the program.

With adults, listening-related problems may take a multitude of forms and may affect various aspects of their personal, social or professional life. Adults often seek our help because they feel tired, depressed or irritable. They may also lack direction or meaning in life or feel unable to adapt to new situations, or to function well under pressure.The efficacy of sound stimulation was demonstrated in a group of adult stutters. [7]

Others are interested in the sound stimulation for professional reasons. We are often approached by singers who start losing their voice; businesspeople who have difficulty following conversations when several people speak at once; salespeople who cannot articulate clearly and therefore "lose" their clients' attention; artists and writers suffering from a "creative block;" students who cannot complete their dissertations. And the list goes on and on....

The listening training program is also used to enhance a skill. It helps people to learn a foreign language or to work on their accent. Music students often come to us wanting to improve their singing voice or instrument playing; students in performing arts want to work on their voice quality and oral expression; dancers seek fluidity and ease of body movements; golf or tennis players and other athletes look for visual motor coordination; graphic artists want better appreciation of colors and conceptualization of space.... Many adults come to the program "just to get their battery charged," as they put it.

The sound stimulation can also help elderly people who want to maintain or improve their level of energy and sense of balance. It helps those who wish to maintain an active and fulfilling life. It maximizes their listening even if their hearing starts betraying them.

This list of applications of the sound stimulation program is by no means exhaustive. As we will see in the second and third parts of the book, listening has far-reaching implications for us, and by working on our listening, we can enrich and improve our lives.

Listening

I had spent all night on a plane between Toronto and Geneva. I was tired and jetlagged, waiting for the connecting flight. I distractedly watched the airline staff who were becoming fidgety for some reason; there were fewer and fewer passengers waiting and the loudspeakers would not shut up — their incessant messages kept ringing in my ears. I was surprised I had to wait so long to get my connection, when suddenly I realized that I was the only one left in the waiting room. Beginning to worry, I came up to the airline desk only to find out that they had called my name at least three times and the airplane doors were already closed. So much for the "good listener" I am supposed to be!

Listening is the ability to tune in on sound messages and to tune out at will; a listening problem is the inability to do it well, if at all. But how does listening work? What role is assigned to the ear and to the brain in the process? It took Dr. Tomatis twenty-five years to answer these questions.[1]

ALFRED TOMATIS

Alfred Tomatis was born in Nice in the south of France, on January 1, 1920. He studied at the Faculté de Médecine in Paris and specialized in otolaryngology — the medicine of the ear, nose and throat (ENT).[2]

As he was the son of an opera singer, his first clients in private practice were opera singers suffering from voice problems. These performers were often at the very peak of their careers. At the same time — in the late 1940s, at the request of the French health department — Tomatis was involved in a study of the effect of excessive noise on the hearing of factory workers.[3] During the course of this study, he noticed that the voices of workers who had partial hearing were affected by their hearing loss. The tone of their voice was lower and their speech was poorly articulated. His opera singer clients were afflicted with similar symptoms. This prompted Tomatis to test the ears of his singers, only to discover that they suffered from a hearing loss similar to that of the workers. Following up on that finding, he realized that their hearing loss was due to the "excessive noise" of their own voice.

> Upon studying the auditory control of the voice further, Tomatis concluded that it is the ear that, in connection with the brain, controls voice production. This was summarized in a phrase "We sing with our ear."

Upon studying the auditory control of the voice further, Tomatis concluded that it is the ear that, in connection with the brain, controls voice production. The larynx simply does what it is told to do. This was summarized in a phrase "We sing with our ear," and was later refined as "the voice only contains harmonics the ear is likely to hear." This phenomenon was demonstrated in an experiment before the Académie Nationale de Médecine, and later before the Académie des Sciences, both in Paris, and given the name the Tomatis Effect.[4]

Tomatis's own clinical observations, corroborated

by extensive research using various experimental techniques, led him to the conclusion that there was a marked difference between voice quality when controlled with the right versus the left ear, the right ensuring much better quality. Tomatis named the right ear the "leading ear" because it was the one most adapted for the control of the singing voice, instrument playing, speech production and ear tuning in general, as he later came to discover.

> There seemed to be a particular way of hearing associated with an active involvement with music, which Tomatis named the "musical ear."

As Tomatis examined the various audiograms of the factory workers and the opera singers, a very consistently shaped auditory curve began to emerge.[5] This ascending shape was specific to opera singers and only to those factory workers who were involved in some kind of musical activity. In other words, there seemed to be a particular way of hearing associated with an active involvement with music, which Tomatis named the "musical ear."[6] Hearing was always thought of in quantitative terms — whether one could or could not hear, and if not, to what extent. And now, for the first time, a qualitative aspect — *how* one could hear, or a way of hearing — was introduced into the notion of audition. Further studies of the musical ear showed that there was a way of hearing particular to a specific voice range: there was a "baritone ear," a "soprano ear," etc. Musicians turned out to have their own "ears"— the "violinist ear," the "cellist ear," or the "oboe player ear."

To help opera singers recover their voice, Tomatis created an electronic device. The filters of the device were set so as to simulate the shape of the musical ear, and imposing that way of hearing on the singers by means of headphones gave them back their voice. However, as soon as the headphones were off, the problem returned. A means of maintaining a good quality voice without the constant help of the headphones had to be found — and eventually was. The successive improvements of the machine, which came to be known as the Electronic Ear, reflect an evolution of Tomatis's understanding of the functioning of the ear. The Electronic Ear is now an ear training device — the centerpiece of the Tomatis Method. Tomatis defines it as a "simulator of high quality listening."

Ecstatic about the results of the ear training, the singers spread the good news and all sorts of people affected with all sorts of ailments began to arrive at Dr. Tomatis's office. He found that what applied to the role of the ear in singing also applied to talking.

Not only were there different ways of hearing different voices or musical instruments, but also for different languages and even accents. There exists a sort of "acoustic geography," which makes a "French ear" different from a "Spanish ear," or a "British English ear" different from a "North American ear." That is one of the main reasons why learning a new language is often difficult, since a "foreign" way of hearing is imposed on us. We are made to listen to sounds we are normally "deaf" to. Foreigners have an accent because they talk a new language, while controlling their speech with the ear of their mother tongue.

Students who have gone through the ear training program to help them learn English as a second language not only assimilated it faster and more easily, but also improved in other areas in school. Parents and teachers commented on better reading, spelling, writing and learning in general. These improvements were reflected in higher marks.

It took Dr. Tomatis several years to understand and accept these reports. During this time he studied the mechanisms of written language and the learning process, while continuing to collect increasingly conclusive results with the school-age children he was helping.[7] From there, his field of clinical investigation spread to social adjustment and emotional problems, and to the more extreme cases of communication disorders such as autism.

From voice, to speech, to language, to communication — a logical progression could be seen when considered from the perspective of the ear. But what ear are we talking about? What does a "way of hearing" really mean?

THE ACTIVE EAR

At the request of the French health department, Tomatis started studying the hearing of factory workers exposed to loud noise. He had a hard time winning their trust at first. Back then, it was uncommon for doctors to visit factories. So it is hardly surprising that when he first arrived, the workers were afraid of getting fired if anything was found to be wrong. Later on, when the results were made public, people were satisfied that Tomatis was on their side after all. When rumours of attractive compensatory pensions for those who suffered a hearing loss began to circulate, many workers volunteered to have their hearing retested. Upon retesting, it looked as if the hearing of the workers had all of a sudden deteriorated. It was so much worse that it looked as if there was some cheating going on, even though Tomatis knew that the tests could not be willingly falsified. The anxiety of being "caught" with a hearing problem was replaced by the desire to show one, hence such a difference in the results. Tomatis concluded that the workers were "cheating in good faith." Do you remember the expression "no one is more deaf than he who refuses to hear?" It applies perfectly here.

In the years to follow, Tomatis would repeatedly observe how the auditory function can fluctuate with emotional states, just like the "cheating" workers. Was the ear an active instrument? The discovery of specific ways of hearing — the musical ear, the English ear, etc.

— and the fact that these ways of hearing could be improved and modified with the Electronic Ear went hand in hand with the "emotional" aspect of the ear. Everything pointed to the fact that there was indeed an active side to hearing; the ear could be wonderfully flexible in adapting to a wide range of situations.

Tomatis was confronted with an increasing dilemma. On the one hand, the ear appeared to lead a life of its own, reacting to feelings and adapting to its sound environment — to the sounds of language in particular. On the other hand, according to what he learned in medical school, the ear was not much more than a sort of microphone receiving sounds and transforming them into messages to be sent to the brain. While the traditional physiology of hearing described the ear as an essentially passive instrument, all the evidence brought Tomatis to view it as an active system and offer his own explanation of how it works.

> While the traditional physiology of hearing described the ear as an essentially passive instrument, all the evidence brought Tomatis to view it as an active system and offer his own explanation of how it works.

THE LISTENING MUSCLES

In vision, there are two mechanisms operating. One permits visual perception, allowing us to see. The other makes focusing possible, thanks to the mobility of ocular globes and the adaptation of the pupils. This allows us to look, or not look, at a particular object.

Auditory phenomena indicating a "focusing" quality — such as auditory processing, auditory discrimination or attention span — are usually explained at the level of the brain. It is assumed that the ear passes all the information on to the brain and it is the brain that makes the selection. Certainly, the brain makes the ultimate decision, but why would it not "ask" the ear to be part of the selection process, just like converging ocular globes of the eye in vision? In other words, why would the brain not actively involve the ear in focusing

— or more appropriately — in attuning to sounds?

The traditional description of hearing explains the passive part of sound perception — what corresponds to seeing in vision — and assigns an active role to the ear in only exceptional situations. When exposed to extremely loud sounds, the ear protects itself with the help of two tiny muscles located in the middle ear.[8] They are the hammer muscle, or tensor tympani, and the stirrup muscle, or stapedius. (See Middle Ear.) When sounds are dangerously loud, the hammer muscle attenuates the vibration of the eardrum, and the stirrup muscle acts on the oval window to diminish the intensity of the incoming sound vibrations.

The role of these middle ear muscles has been limited to such extreme situations, although recent findings suggest that they are much more important than previously thought. In particular, some audiologists are recognizing that the stirrup muscle facilitates sound discrimation.[9] These findings add wind to Tomatis' sails, since for more than twenty years he has attributed a broader and much more systematic role to these two muscles — thanks to them we can make use of our "auditory zoom." Since most of us are mainly visual, even when dealing with the auditory, let's use "zoom" as a metaphor in trying to understand how our ear focuses on, or more literally attunes to, sounds.

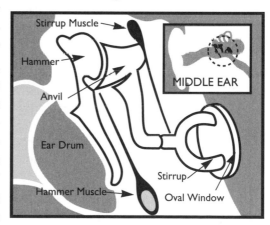

Do you remember the concept of the "French ear"? What it means is that the French can attune perfectly well within the frequency range of the French language; they can automatically zoom in on what they want. But this zoom is not at all adapted to another language, for example English — thus the accent, and the difficulty learning it. It would require some training to adjust the zoom, to make it focus on the new sound range. But a young child exposed to both French and English becomes bilingual, because early in life this zoom is not yet limited to a specific sound range. In children, the ear is open and ready to be attuned to any surrounding sounds. Musicians often come from a background of musicians, probably because their ear has "always" been exposed to music — making their zoom embrace the full range of the musical ear.

Giving an attuning role to the middle ear muscles does not exclude their traditionally assigned role of protection against loud noises. To attune to the sounds we want automatically implies cutting off the unwanted ones. That is what happens when we try to converse in a noisy environment. This double role of the middle ear muscles is perfectly illustrated by a mother who can easily sleep in a very noisy room but will wake up at the faintest babble of her baby. The child, whose ear is wide open for language integration, is also extremely sensitive to noises. His zoom open — his listening skills not yet developed — the protection system is still fragile. The paradox of poor listening is that it also means hearing too much.[10]

This new, unorthodox conception of how the ear works follows the model of vision. The first part of the process — the perception of sound — is hearing. The second part — the attuning to sound — is the way of hearing or listening. The middle ear muscles are, therefore, the "listening muscle."

Tomatis remarks that the stirrup muscle is the only one in the body that is in a constant state of tension; it is

> How the ear works follows the model of vision. The first part of the process — the perception of sound — is hearing. The second part — the attuning to sound — is the way of hearing or listening.

always working.[11] And because it never rests, we have a chance to rest ourselves. It provides not only protection from external noises, but from internal noises as well. Cover your ears with your hands, or put your ear against someone else's body. Doing this will give you a faint idea of the constant roaring noise our body makes from the inside. And despite this, we can experience silence. The middle ear muscles act as a kind of watchdog or guardian angel; they protect our sleep but also wake us up when necessary.

The Electronic Ear exercises these attuning muscles by means of sound stimulations — sounds of one's voice or of an external source. More exactly, when the sound information goes through one channel — the one which induces passive hearing — the muscles are relaxed. Passing to the second channel — the one which induces the correct way of hearing stimulates the two muscles. This passage from one channel to another, repeated over and over again, gives a real workout to these smallest and most difficult to reach muscles of the body; it provides training in listening.

> Listening is the active focusing and protecting function of the ear that permits us to receive what we want and reject what we don't want.

Listening is the active focusing and protecting function of the ear that permits us to receive what we want and reject what we don't want. To explain listening to younger children and their parents, I ask them to think of a comic strip character with a hand that comes out of his ear to grab the sounds he wants. And isn't that the way most younger children draw people — with arms sticking out of their head? Another analogy of the ear's role in listening is a frog flicking its tongue to catch a fly.

LINKS BETWEEN LISTENING AND VOICE

Tomatis points out that the same nerves that control the middle ear muscles are also involved in voice production.

The facial nerve innervates the muscles of the face, including those of the lips, which are so important for the clarity of voice and the intelligibility of speech. The

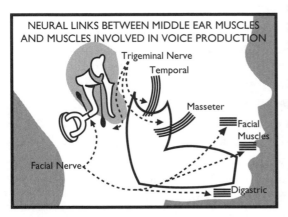

same nerve also influences the stirrup muscle. This "ear-face link" is intuitively understood by experienced teachers who can "read" whether students are listening or not from the expression on their face. The facial nerve is also in charge of the digastric muscle, which permits the opening of the mouth. The other important link between the ear and the mouth is the trigeminal nerve, which is connected to the hammer listening muscle, as well as the muscles that enable us to chew and close our mouths, the masseter and temporal muscles. This nerve is yet another direct link between listening and the voice. If yawning is one way to avoid listening, tightly closing the jaw is another. When a child clenches his teeth in anger while being told something, you know very well that your words are falling on deaf ears. (See figure)

This double neural link between the ear and the voice seems consistent with the recent findings that the middle ear muscles are somehow activated when we use our voice.[9]

HEART TO THE LEFT. LANGUAGE TO THE RIGHT

Early on in his work, Tomatis had discovered the "leading" role of the right ear in the control of voice. He then realized that weak or non-existent control by the leading ear was often associated with language, reading and learning problems, and that it also affected instrument playing. The left ear simply does not seem to have the same quality of control.

Why is the right ear the leading one? This may have something to do with where our heart is. Because our heart is on the left, the left recurrent nerve connecting the brain with the larynx has to make a detour in its path, whereas the right nerve follows a much more direct and therefore shorter path. The majority of the nerves leading from the brain cross to the other side of the body. Thus the left side of the brain is connected with the right side of the larynx via the shorter right recurrent nerve. (See Recurrent Nerves figure.)

From the time children emit their very first sounds, they realize that not only can they perceive sounds but also they can monitor their production. They start playing with their voice, and as the ear picks up the sounds, they repeat them again

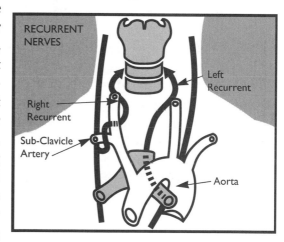

and again, "echoing" themselves. This sounding game is the starting-point of attuning the auditory zoom to their own voice. When the voice control becomes more precise — when the zoom is attuned enough — the sounds are only repeated twice: *ma-ma*, *da-da*, *pipi* — this is the babbling phase of language development. For Tomatis, this double response is nothing more than the neural impulse coming from the brain to the larynx at two different times. As you remember, the right recurrent nerve is shorter. Therefore it delivers its impulse first, soon followed by the impulse carried by the left nerve.

We know that the right ear has more connections

with the left side of the brain than the left ear. We also know now that the neural link between the left brain and the larynx is shorter. Therefore, the ear-to-brain-to-larynx-back-to-ear control loop is more direct for the right ear. That may explain why the right ear is the most efficient zoom for the voice control and other incoming sounds. And if all goes well, the right ear becomes the leading, the listening ear.

But if for some reason the right ear is not in a position to assume this control, it will either be picked up by the left ear or a listening dominance will not take place at all — there will be no leading ear. In both cases, hesitant and monotonous speech may occur, possibly stammering or even stuttering. In most children with language and learning problems the right ear did not develop as the leading ear.

Ear infections at this vital stage of language development may be responsible for the right ear failing to assume control. This failure may also be a response to an unpleasant environment: there may be too much noise, too much tension, or too many conflicts. Failing to establish right ear control is one way for the child to protect himself. Avoiding using the shortest track introduces a distance between the outside world and the child while not cutting listening off completely. This is a way of making a compromise. You may want to be alone, but you are hungry, so you sit with others at the dinner table. However, only your body is present: your ear and mind are somewhere else. This is an everyday reality for many children.

Tomatis suggests that the anatomical asymmetry of the right and left recurrent nerves may not only make the right ear the leading ear for listening, but may also be one of the reasons why the left hemisphere becomes the part of the brain that controls language. By using the shorter "right ear – left brain – larnyx – right ear" loop from a very early age, the child may also provide more stimulation to the right side of his body. This could explain why 90 percent of the population is right-handed. Animals as well as humans develop a dominance to perform voluntary acts. Only human beings exhibit this overwhelmingly right-sided preference. Perhaps it is the language function which is right-sided and language simply uses the body to express the mind.

It may also be no coincidence that we use the heart as a metaphor to describe non-verbal qualities such as empathy and intuition. These are qualities usually linked with right-brain activity. We talk of being good-hearted, wearing ones heart on one's sleeve or following one's heart.

While hypothetical, this explanation of brain dominance and right-sidedness is well worth further investigation. I have found in my clinical practice that children with language delays or impairments, or without any language whatsoever — such as children with deafness, Down's Syndrome, or autism — show a higher incidence of mixed dominance. This is also true of learning disabled children.

The Electronic Ear is equipped with a system that permits preferential stimulation of the right ear by decreasing the volume of sound coming to the left ear. As a listening trainer, I have had numerous opportunities to observe the effect establishing right-ear dominance has on voice production, speech fluency, as well as language acquisition and learning ability.

Is being left-handed a problem? Relying on my clinical experience, I don't think so, except for the fact that living in a right-handed world means being a minority with everything this implies in our society. What I have observed is that problems arise when there is a *mixed* lateral dominance; that is, when neither the right nor the left side does the job well. Right-handed people who listen on the left — and speak to the left —as I did and as do many dyslexic and other learning disabled children, may present more problems than left-handed people who speak and listen "on the right."

The Listening Test

Since his early work with singers and workers, Tomatis had realized that an audiogram offered much more information than just the nature and severity of a hearing loss. It was in looking at an audiogram that he first identified a curve that was to be known as "the musical ear." Years of reading tests between the lines resulted in a huge wealth of information. This included information about ways of hearing, voice quality, language acquisition, learning ability, etc. The fact that test results could vary with emotional states — as in the case of the worried workers — added a psychological dimension to the test.

The Test was continuously modified to respond to new diagnostic needs. Tomatis saw more and more people whose hearing was normal but who had listening problems. Little by little, the audiogram disappeared from Dr. Tomatis's practice and gave way to what is now the number one assessment tool of the Method — the Listening Test.

Among other things, the Listening Test can provide valuable information about the energy level, posture, muscle tensions, balance, motor functions and other body-related functions. I will talk more about these in later chapters.

• • •

Tomatis's explanation of the mechanisms of the ear is based on known and described phenomena: the active role of the middle ear muscles, the common innervation of both the ear and the face, the asymmetry of the recurrent nerve. In other words, the facts themselves are not new; what is new is their interpretation. This is typical of how Tomatis revises well-established theories and their applications. His revision of the traditional theory of hearing and the emergence of the Listening Test from the audiogram are cases in point.

Sound and Movement

One day an acquaintance of mine who is a singer burst into my office as if coming on stage. His presence filled the room. He carried himself well, with a smile and a sparkle in his eyes. Making a grand gesture with his arms, he declared in a deep, vibrant voice, "Paul, I need your help. I am so depressed!"

I would have thought he was joking, had I not known about the turmoil he was currently experiencing in his life. Yes, he had problems, yes he was truly suffering, and yes, he needed help, but his voice and body blatantly contradicted his own diagnosis — he was going through a hard time but this had nothing to do with depression. And in a few weeks he was back on top of the world where he belonged.

I have already talked about one of the things the ear does in addition to hearing: it acts as a control mechanism for the voice in singing as well as speaking. This is illustrated by the rich "texture" of my friend's voice. His physical appearance and his boisterous manner demonstrate two other basic roles of the ear: The ear as harmoniser of body functions and as provider of energy to the brain. The ear is involved in both the "tuning" and the "energizing" of our body and mind. In this chapter I will examine the links between the ear and the body and their influence in the course of our lives.

THE BODY HAS ITS EAR

Let's take a closer look at the appearance of my baritone friend. His impressive physical presence, his gait, his upright posture with the chest expanded, his wide, expressive, forever smiling face — these are all characteristics found in many opera singers.

> The ear is involved in both the "tuning" and the "energizing" of our body and mind.

Can they be attributed to their training and to the grand style required to perform opera? Maybe, but only to some extent.

When Tomatis started working with singers who had lost their voices, he observed that they also lost their posture — they started to slouch, their chests would shrink. Then, when the ear was stimulated with the Electronic Ear, all of a sudden the body straightened up, the thorax widened and the incredible capacity for deep breathing returned. These changes came hand in hand with voice improvement, and with an increase of the singer's overall energy level.

In working with children who have difficulties with schoolwork, I consistently observe that better listening not only leads to progress in reading and spelling, but also improves their balance, coordination and motor functions. Some start riding a bicycle, others do better in hockey, tennis, baseball or dance.... Their handwriting no longer looks like chicken scratches. Parents often comment that their child is now tidier and more organized. They have a better awareness of time and space. Some finally learn to tell time, others have no more problems differentiating the right from the left, and the list goes on.

Children with cerebral palsy provide another example of body posture improving with listening training. The comment I most often hear from their parents and therapists is that the children have better control of the verticality of their trunk and neck following a sound stimulation program. These kids can now hold their heads straight up, rather than rest them on their shoulders.

These examples indicate that there are indeed direct links between sounds, the ear and the body. Thus, stimulating the ear not only affects voice and language, it also "shapes" the body, changes its position, coordinates its movements and refines the motor functions. Attuning listening induces an attuning of the entire body. While these results appear rather surprising at first glance, a brief review of the functions of the inner ear resolves the mystery.

THE INNER EAR

Entirely embedded in bone, the labyrinth of the inner ear is made up of two parts. One is the cochlea, which looks like a snail and contains the Corti cells. Its function is sound perception. The second part is the vestibular system, which is made up of two cavities and three tubes. The cavities are called the sacculus and the utriculus, and the tubes are the semicircular canals, which allow us to perceive the three dimensions of space. The inner part of the vestibular system is covered with sensory hair cells and is filled with fluid. When head and body move — and the labyrinth with them — this fluid follows at a different pace, and this difference in speed of movement will stimulate the sensory cells. The resulting neural impulse is sent to the vestibular

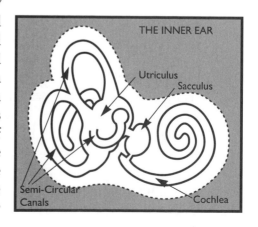

THE INNER EAR

Utriculus

Sacculus

Semi-Circular Canals

Cochlea

nerve, which carries the message to the brain. These vestibular sensations record body positions and movements, permitting their control.

Because of their apparently distinct functions — the cochlea perceiving sounds and the vestibular system registering movements — these two mechanisms are usually viewed as two distinct entities. While the cochlea is studied by specialists of audition, the vestibular system is of interest to physical and occupational therapists as well as experts in the field of agravitation — the study of life in the absence of gravity. The cochlea and the vestibular system are seldom united as they are in the body.

SOUND IS MOVEMENT

In his usual way, Tomatis takes well known facts and interprets them in light of the results he obtained while "tickling" the ears, as he jokingly describes his training by sound stimulation. For him, the cochlea and the vestibular system have the same role. They both help us to perceive movements. The vestibular system is in charge of the slower movements — those that we see, feel and call movements. The cochlea specializes in faster oscillatory movements — those that we don't see and can hardly feel, but those we hear. Let's take an example. When a bird flies, we can see the slow movements of its wings, but we usually don't hear them. But we hear the much faster movements of the wings of a flying bee. Reaching a certain speed — sixteen to twenty vibrations, or cycles (Hertz) per seconds — a movement starts to be perceived as a sound. The faster the vibration, the higher pitched the sound. This passage from one mode of perception to another is not clear-cut: there is a transition zone where it is difficult to tell if we feel a vibration or hear a sound. The ear can perceive sounds up to about 20,000 Hertz, or up to 20,000 movements per second.

The cochlear-vestibular system of the inner ear must be viewed as a single apparatus doing one job — analyzing movements — and not as two different entities with separate functions. It can be compared to a double-ended antenna with its vestibular end receiving the slower information of the motions and positions of the body, and the cochlear end receiving the faster ones, such as the sounds of our voice and of the environment. To simplify things, from now on I will call the vestibular end of the antenna the "ear of the body" and the cochlear one, the "auditory ear." This double antenna largely contributes to our awareness and communication with our own body — our body image — as well as our awareness and communication with the world around us through the dimensions of time and space.

The notion of space comes from the ear of the body, which includes an ingenious three-dimensional compass. The ear also introduces the notion of time. Let me explain. In vision, all of the information reaches our eyes at the same time; we see the whole picture at once. But it is an entirely different story when it comes to sounds. Imagine if we were to hear the entire tune all at once! A time factor is absolutely necessary: a tune has to last a certain period of time to be sung or heard. And it is this quality of sound production and perceptions monitored by the ear that brings the "time dimension" into the realm of the auditory.

> Music is made up of rhythm and melody. It involves both ends of the antenna — the ear of the body and the auditory ear.

As a youngster, I remember feeling lost in time and space — "timed out" and "spaced out," as I called it. This problem greatly improved when my listening came alive, but it did not disappear altogether. I am still quite absentminded. I attribute this problem partly to a poor awareness of time and space. I have difficulty "listening to time and space." The episode at the airport is a typical example.

Music: Sound-Movement Harmony

Music is made up of rhythm and melody. It involves both ends of the antenna — the ear of the body and the auditory ear. This is illustrated by some types of music — dance music in particular — that induce very specific movements in the body. Try to tango to a rap tune, or rock'n'roll to a waltz, and you will feel the power that some types of music have over your body. Your strong muscles and powerful mind can hardly go against the "will" of these molecules dancing all around you, which your brain interprets as sounds.

While the purpose of military music has very little to do with dancing, there is a similarity in the use of rhythms to induce specific body movements. You cannot help but walk forward in a straight line to a military march, while a waltz makes you want to circle around and around.

How can music induce body movements? We remember that our perception of all body movements comes from the fluid stimulating the sensory cells inside the vestibular system. But can't certain types of sounds induce movements of the fluid filling the inner ear, which will be picked up by the vestibular system? As the cochlea and the vestibular system are connected and are both filled and immersed in the same types of fluid, it seems a reasonable explanation. This accounts for the well-known fact that we are all physically speaking, "moved" by music.

Music engages and reinforces the "dialogue" between the ear of the body and the auditory ear. This dialogue is important for the acquisition of motor functions, verticality, space and time awareness, lateral dominance and language. One of the purposes of singing nursery rhymes to children is to attune these two "ears" — to make them both listen — to prepare the path for the integration of words, phrases and numbers. Harmony between movements and sounds — between the body and the auditory — is a prerequisite for the acquisition of language and for academic learning in general. This is why music should play an essential part in early and in preschool life. (See Chapters 8, 9 and 10.) For this reason, nursery rhymes and other children's songs are an integral part of the program of sound stimulation for younger children and for children with delayed or absent language.

Other researchers and clinicians have also indicated the existence of a link between the vestibular system, body posture, language acquisition and learning ability. The pioneering work of de Quiros in Argentina,[2] and of Jean Ayres[3], deserve a mention, as well as the more recent work of Levinson.[4] The uniqueness of Tomatis is in his conception of a "dialogue" between the body and the auditory ears.

Clinical implications of this ear-body relationship and of the effects of sound stimulation are endless. It can help singers to improve their posture and breathing, musicians to refine the precision and dexterity of their instrument playing, and dancers to add more expression to their movements. Athletes perfect their performance and public speakers are able to better harmonize what they say with the way they say it; they gain better control of their body language. I already mentioned some of the changes most commonly observed in youngsters with learning problems. For most, sound stimulation provides what I could best describe as an inner massage which, apart from relaxation, has been described by clients of The Listening Centre as being "in touch with myself," "together," "with my feet firmly planted on the ground."

> Harmony between movements and sounds — between the body and the auditory — is a prerequisite for the acquisition of language and for academic learning in general.

THE ROCKING BOAT

When I explain to youngsters, their parents, teachers or therapists how a problem of the ear of the body can be at the base of difficulties at school, I like to use the following analogy. Having a vestibular problem makes one unstable in one's own body. It is like trying to carry on all the normal activities of life on a rocking boat in a most unpredictable sea.

First, this creates a degree of clumsiness, a feeling of being ill at ease in one's own body — the sense of being "off," particularly when in a group. Some youngsters are able to hide this inner discomfort, but it brings about shyness and complexes about physical appearance or withdrawal. Sometimes, the awkwardness is not just felt inside, it shows on the outside too: the youngster tends to look and act "weird," as his peers may say. Other kids may poke fun at him by pushing him around or else ignoring him. Of course, he will react. Reactions may vary from acting as a clown (playing weird is one way to live with discomfort), to belonging to the gang of the "bad guys" where all that is "bad" is admissible. In this case, the child with a vestibular problem is usually the first one to be caught as he is too clumsy to make a quick escape. Small wonder that he may wind-up being aggressive, angry, antisocial or rebellious.

I frequently see youngsters who have been labeled "emotionally disturbed," or having "behavior and social adjustment problems." Often these children have been bounced from one therapy, one special program or one institution to another. My first thought is always: "Let's get them off this rocking boat first, and then we'll see what's left of their social adjustment-behavioral-emotional thing."

Let's go back now to our zoom analogy. What would happen if you wanted to take pictures from the deck of a rocking boat? Of course it would be possible, but it would require a great deal of concentration, and many of the pictures might still be out of focus and badly centered. Language acquisition and learning are in many ways similar to taking pictures or filming.

One needs to take correct aim in time and space at the relevant information, to focus and to attune well, and to use both the ear of the body and the auditory ear to "catch" the messages. In other words, listening requires not only a high precision of the auditory zoom, but also stability of the tripod — the ear of the body.

Is it surprising, then, that a child with such a "rocking-boat problem" returns from school exhausted, complaining of headaches and hating studying? This is what happens to John. Reading and learning at school make him feel seasick. Hard to believe? Well, have you tried to read in a car on a bumpy road? If you have, then you understand why he did not even open the captivating storybook his aunt gave him for his birthday and why he did not thank her.

Those who think that John's struggle with reading is due to some kind of visual-perceptual problem should know that the ocular muscles, those which make the eyes move, are linked with the vestibular system. Thus, the decoding of the words in reading is controlled by the ear of the body as well. And the reading problem seldom comes alone. John fidgets a lot, his attention span is short; the word "hyperactive" may have been used by some to describe him. These are all signs of inadequate functioning of the ear of the body. He hates sports and often gets into trouble with the other kids. When he gets older, he may also show signs of some of the emotional and social adjustment problems I have previously described. The "rocking boat effect" is one possible listening problem often found with learning disabled or dyslexic children.

WHEN THE ZOOM IS OFF FOCUS

In John's class, there is another boy who has a hard time studying, also diagnosed as dyslexic. His name is Frank. And what a difference there is between Frank and John! Frank is built like an athlete; he is a "sports freak" who wants to be a professional football player. For Frank, sports provide an outlet, an environment in which he may feel successful and comfortable. He is easy going and gets along well with everybody, except that sometimes he has a short temper with the teachers. But they understand his frustration.

As a young child, Frank had one ear infection after another. Despite standing, crawling and walking at a very early age, he was a late talker. When Frank speaks, his voice is low, his speech is mumbled and monotonous; he always uses the same words and expressions, like some of the athletes you see interviewed on TV. While he is doing quite well in math, his reading is poor. His writing looks like a script of his way of talking. Frank suffers from a more common form of dyslexia. His auditory ear is affected — probably because of a history of chronic ear infections — and the delayed language development makes reading and writing difficult. If the sounds of language are perceived in a distorted way, this is how the brain will process them. Therefore, it is normal that the translation of these sounds into graphic form through written language suffers from the same distortions. The good news for Frank is that the ear of the body — the tripod — is perfectly stable. For Frank, the boat is not rocking, it is the zoom that does not work.

John's and Frank's reading and learning problems illustrate a listening weakness at each of the two ends of the antenna — the body end for John and the auditory end for Frank. John is a stranger in his own body, while Frank is a stranger in his own language. As a result, both are strangers to learning at school. Most learning disabilities seem to lie somewhere in between — reflecting a disharmony at both the vestibular and cochlear levels of the ear or a disharmony between the two. I myself was one of these youngsters who had problems with both.

At the beginning of my treatment in Paris, there were a few times when I felt dizzy. Having lived on a rocking boat for as long as I could remember, I was not aware of it anymore. However, when I regained my balance, I could actually feel the rocking again for a few seconds. After a boat trip, it takes all of us a few minutes to readjust to the solid ground under our feet. It was later in the program that I realized that socializing was becoming spontaneous, easy and fun — even in another language! The zoom was beginning to work. Only towards the end did I realize that I could read; the harmony between the two antennae had been established. Learning was now possible.

In previous chapters, I talked about mixed dominance being associated with language and learning difficulties. A problem of lateral dominance can be compared to a lack of dialogue a disharmony or an imbalance — between the right and the left sides of the body. If this affects both the right and left ears of the body, we may have a rocking boat problem similar to John's. When only the auditory ear is involved — as is often the case for right-handed people who are left dominant for listening and speech control — it may be a problem of the zoom such as Frank's. However, a learning-disabled youngster may present either one of these two problems, or a mixture of both with no evidence of mixed dominance. In this case, the difficulty can be traced to the ear itself, or to the neural connections to each "ear" — the auditory or the vestibular pathway. The Listening Test can be indispensable in locating the source of the problem. But it often needs to be complemented by other evaluations, such as neurological or neuro-psychological assessments.

Balance and harmony — conceived by this dialogue between the ear of the body and the auditory ear — are other dimensions of listening. They give us a sense of being at ease, of being on solid ground, of well-being and self-confidence. It is not just the ear and the nervous system but, in fact, the entire body that is involved in listening.

Music  Is Energy

You know that to stand is more tiring than to walk. You also know that, while supposedly energy-consuming, a good walk, a run, or a workout has the opposite effect: it can be most invigorating. There is no better way to start a day than to listen to upbeat music or to sing in the shower. The liveliness of the sounds fills you with vital energy.

Not only do sounds send messages to the brain, but they also carry vital energy as well. Like air and food, sounds nourish the nervous system.

The brain receives and dispatches energy to the body and mind, but cannot generate its own; it is totally dependant on other sources. Of the three main sources of energy, two — air and food — are well known. We can all predict what will happen if we are deprived of either one. It does not take long for the brain to be damaged as a result of asphyxia. Severe malnutrition may provoke brain damage, and we know that a poorly balanced diet has detrimental effects on mental activity.

The third, lesser known source of energy for the brain, is carried by the myriad bits of information constantly stimulating our senses, known as sensory energy.

Sounds and movements generate energy, and the ear acts as a dynamo transforming this energy into neural impulses that it sends to the brain. Based on his clinical experience, Tomatis estimates that, taken as a whole, the ear provides the nervous system with almost 90 per cent of its overall sensory energy.[1] This includes energy coming from sounds — cochlear energy[2] — and from the body movements — vestibular energy. [3]

Symptoms consistently seen in people with weaknesses in the perception of sounds in the high frequency range tend to indicate that these sounds are highly "nutritive" for the brain. These "vitamin-enriched" sounds were named "charging sounds" by Tomatis. The cochlea contains a greater number of Corti cells in the zone receiving these high frequency sounds, which may be one of the reasons for their "charging effect." From the point of view of physics, high frequency means a greater number of vibrations, and therefore, a greater energizing power.

Life Is in the Voice

High frequency sounds make up the higher harmonics, the timbre of the voice. A voice rich or poor in high frequencies should not be confused with a high-or-low-pitched one. One can have a well-timbred but low-pitched voice like many radio and TV announcers, politicians and preachers. The voice of a bass has virtually the same higher harmonic content as that of a tenor. The famous low-pitched "ohm" of the Tibetan monks is extremely rich in higher harmonics.

The unpleasant experience of exposure to unbearable and "unlistenable" high pitched voices may have biased

Throughout the book I use the term "energy" in the same way we use the term "electricity." We knew how to use, store and control electricity long before we found out what it is composed of. It is the same thing for energy. We know it is within us while we are alive and that we lose it when we die; we also, more or less, know what to do to increase or decrease its level. However, attempting to explain *what* it actually is can be another story altogether, and I will not even try to venture into it here.

you against high sounds altogether. You should know that these kinds of voices are so annoying because they are too "narrow," or poor in both low and high frequencies. They are not just annoying because of their high pitch. Paradoxically, they sound high because they are not high enough.

Low-pitched voices with little high frequency content usually sound lifeless, dull and monotonous, rather than low. They carry little "charge" for the brain and consume more energy than they give off, exhausting the speaker. To the listener, they provide little charge to help the ear and brain process the verbal information, thus exhausting him and possibly even putting him to sleep. This kind of voice is typical among fast-growing adolescents who appear to be constantly tired and lethargic. Many depressed people also speak with such a voice.

DOWN THE SPIRAL OF DEPRESSION

One can sometimes follow the progressive shutting out of all sources of sensory stimulation in people with depression, leading to "sensory malnutrition" and in some cases even to "sensory asphyxia." Whatever the cause of depression, the chain of reactions it generates is fairly predictable. Doors and windows stay closed because the mildest draft or the slightest change in temperature is felt as an assault and a health hazard. Curtains should not be open because daylight is so disturbingly bright. What's the use of moving, going out, walking, or exercising? It is all too tiring. Music is either too loud, or too annoying for the ear. Meeting people is out of the question — getting ready, having to listen and talk is too much of a disturbance! All stimulation becomes increasingly bothersome and all action increasingly tiring.

Many people suffering from depression unwillingly put themselves into a state of sensory deprivation by cutting off all sources of sensory energy. This, in turn, weakens their ability to act and react, further increasing the depression and thereby creating a spiral effect.

While the use of hearing plugs is helpful in extreme situations — a noisy club or rock concert — they can be counterproductive if used to isolate oneself from normal sounds or to go to sleep. Not only do they weaken the protecting-focusing function of the listening ear but, in the case of depressive tendencies, they reinforce the spiral effect.

CHANTING AS A REMEDY

Once Dr. Tomatis was called to an abbey where the monks had lost their spirit, some having given up monastic life altogether. Those who stayed were feeling more and more tired; many suffered from all sorts of physical and psychological problems and never left their room. The cultural, social and spiritual "health" of the monastery was at stake.

The monks tried to solve their problem themselves. The first thing they had done was eliminate the night vigil and sleep all night long, believing that a good night's sleep is the best remedy for tiredness. As a result of oversleeping, they became more tired. They then decided to consult various physicians. Each one came, made a diagnosis and wrote out prescriptions. One physician decided that their vegetarian diet was at fault and suggested that they eat meat. The monks were still tired, so vitamins were added to their diet. Then came all sorts of medications. However, the religious men still felt ill and continued to leave the monastery.

When his turn came, Tomatis attacked the problem from the point of view of the ear. He found out that with the changes that occurred after the Second Vatican council of 1960, the monks had decided to stop singing Gregorian chant. They put themselves in a state of sensory deprivation that led to a sort of "collective nervous breakdown," with all the possible side effects that a loss of energy may have on the body, mind and spirit.

The batteries were flat and needed to be recharged. To re-energize the monks, Tomatis recommended the reintroduction of Gregorian chant. It was difficult for many of the monks to follow this suggestion. After all, singing is the last thing you feel like doing when you are depressed. To "awaken" the ear again, a sound stimulation program with the help of the Electronic Ear was suggested for most of the monks. The great majority regained their physical and spiritual health after following the program.[4]

GREGORIAN CHANT

To better realize what happened to these monks, it is important to understand that Benedictine monastic life allows minimal conversation time. Already hardly talking, and with chanting eliminated, the monks hardly used their voices anymore. Thus they lost one of the main sources of sensory energy for the brain; they "starved" it and more proteins and vitamins could not compensate. Normally, Benedictine monks spend six or more hours a day chanting. It is also interesting to note that Gregorian chant is very rich in high frequency sounds, which are energizing.

Gregorian chant is used as part of the Tomatis sound stimulation program. Recordings from the abbey of St. Pierre de Solesmes have been found to be the most effective. This is probably a credit to two monks from Solesmes — Dom Moquereau and Dom Gajard. They each spent about fifty years "purifying" the chant from the many influences it received over time, and rediscovered how it was sung in the twelfth century. [5]

Gregorian chant has other healing qualities besides "charging" of the brain. It does not have a tempo, or a preimposed beat. Instead, its rhythm is induced by physiological rhythms, such as the respiration and heartbeat of a rested, relaxed person. Gregorian chant gives energy and inner peace to those who chant and those who listen. It keeps the body and mind in a state of calm awakening.[6] A vocal technique that borrows from Gregorian chant is introduced in the Earobic exercises of Part III.

Sacred chants are strikingly similar in different cultures and religions. The same elements are found in all of them: incantations, repetitiveness, lack of tempo and rich higher harmonic content. They are all variations of the same vocal techniques, sharing a common purpose.

FILTERED MUSIC

Since the beginning of humanity, music has accompanied man. Hunting tools and musical instruments are among the first man-made objects. Considering the "enlightening" role of Gregorian chant during the obscure Middle Ages, one can stretch the role of music further to say that it provided the necessary nutrient for man to move on, transcend himself and take charge of his own evolution. Music has certainly played a key role in the development of consciousness and creativity, two unique qualities of the human species. Music fulfills a human need as fundamental as the need to eat. Thus it accompanies and supports man in the struggle for evolution.

Hippocrates, the father of Western medicine, brought his patients to the temple to make them listen to music. Since then, music and medicine have taken separate paths, until recent years when there has been a new surge in the healing dimension of music. This is in part due to the renewed belief that some types of music can provide a powerful therapeutic tool. Thus, the advent of numerous educational, remedial and relaxation techniques known as music therapies. In the context of the sound stimulation program, music can help those clients

> Music has certainly played a key role in the development of consciousness and creativity, two unique qualities of the human species. Music fulfills a human need as fundamental as the need to eat. Thus it accompanies and supports man in the struggle for evolution.

who do not use their voice as a source of sensory stimulation because of low energy or poor voice quality.

The music of Handel, Teleman, Paganini, Mozart and Vivaldi was originally used in the program to provide sensory stimulation. Pieces played by instruments in the higher harmonics, such as violin, trumpet and flute were favoured. Later, electronic filters were used to eliminate the low frequency sounds and retain only the higher harmonics — a technique Tomatis was already using to modify voices in his work on sound perception before birth. The result was a concentration of charging sounds that we call "filtered music."

UNIVERSAL MOZART

Having listened to filtered Mozart during my own sound stimulation program, and having used it to help virtually every client I've seen in my twenty years of practice, I am still amazed by its universal qualities. People of all ages enjoy it — from young hyperactive children to apathetic teenagers, from overworked executives to free spirits. I once saw an autistic child who rejected all physical contact, as is common with such children.

> The music of Mozart relaxes the overly active and the anxious and energies the tired and the depressed.

Refusing to put the headphones on, but keen on hearing the music, he solved the dilemma by cupping his hand and thereby capturing sound as if he was bringing fresh water to his ear. It took him a few days to come to terms with the fact that the only way he could enjoy the music was to wear the headphones. Paradoxically, the few who do not enjoy Mozart's filtered music are musicians. This dislike has more to do with filtering than with Mozart's music. Their resistance is in fact a tribute to the great composer. As the Québécois singer and poet Gilles Vigneault once jokingly told me, "With your filters, you assassinate Mozart!"

The universal appeal of Mozart goes far beyond the clients of The Listening Centre. In all "primitive" societies where different Western music is introduced, the music of Mozart is the only one that is always accepted.

The consistent results obtained during the sound stimulation program with the use of Mozart provide another example of its universal quality. His music is the only one we know that creates a perfect balance between the charging effect and a sense of calmness and well-being. It relaxes the overly active and the anxious and energizes the tired and the depressed.[7]

Why does Mozart have such a universal appeal? I have no scientific answers to this questions, just thoughts. The precocious musical inclinations of Mozart are a legend. He started playing the clavier when he was barely three, before he had fully assimilated language, and he wrote notes before words. At that time, his "listening zoom" had not yet become conditioned to focus specifically on the sounds of his own language. Having such a wide open capacity for listening may have allowed him to play instruments and, a little later, to compose music inspired by his own inner rhythms.

It is interesting to note that Mozart as a child lived and played in most of the countries of Europe and did not seem to have any problems attracting audiences who spoke languages other than his native German. Mozart was "beyond language," a quality most children share with him, and his music conveys this youth and spontaneity.

I also believe that Mozart himself was the first to benefit from the healing effects of his music. "Mozart composed music of radiant vivacity, sparkle, and wit at times when he was crushed by neglect, debt, and the awful discouragement of living his whole life insufficiently compensated and recognized," notes one of his biographers.[8]

ENERGY FOR THE BODY

Physical, occupational and movement therapists are probably the health care practitioners who make the most use of the energizing effect of sensory stimulations in a clinical setting. Through different kinds of massage techniques, music and voice, different lights and odors, they stimulate the nervous system using our senses. Through rocking, rolling and other movements, they give a privileged place to stimulation of the vestibular system — the ear of the body.

The listening program uses sounds as physical therapy uses movement. This makes it a preferred alternative for those who are unable to move freely for some physical, genetic or neurological reason. In the absence of body movements, the vestibular system has no chance of being stimulated. In turn, this lack of stimulation worsens the condition. Among those who may benefit are people who suffer from some form of brain damage that may have delayed or impaired motor development, premature children who had little tactile contact in the incubator, or children with Down's syndrome who typically have poor muscle tone. Children who are partially or completely paralysed by a form of cerebral palsy, or those who have suffered a head injury or a stroke may also benefit from this treatment.

Physiological changes most commonly observed in the above-mentioned situations are: improved balance, better posture, deeper respiration and more precision in movement. At the level of the voice, articulation becomes easier and speech becomes clearer and more intelligible. The improved body control and higher level of energy also help people focus their attention and concentrate for longer periods of time. This is extremely important for the successful outcome of traditional interventions such as physical or speech therapy, and for integration into the school system.

Children with Down's syndrome respond particularly well to the energizing effect of Mozart. Their improved muscle tone is reflected in better posture and facial expression. The child is able to keep his mouth closed with his tongue in. His speech also becomes more intelligible.[9]

Sound stimulation can help children with cerebral palsy. They appear to be more at ease and peaceful with their body, as if they better accept it despite its limitations. One of the consequences of this change is greater motivation to actively participate in the lengthy and sometimes painful therapies that are required.

Valerie Dejean, an occupational therapist of the Spectrum Center in Bethesda, MD, has developed programs that combine sound stimulation and sensory integration techniques mainly for children with autism, development disorders and cerebral palsy. I am so convinced by the efficacy of such a multisensory approach that I've started to encourage The Listening Centre to move in that direction.

The two ends of the listening ear's antenna supply the brain with information and the energy necessary to process this information. This is a lesser known, but no less fundamental role of listening. Listening is an amazingly sophisticated skill at the junction of the body and mind. Its primary role is to keep us communicating and in tune with the world. This is why the desire to use this skill to communicate is critical for growth and proper functioning of listening.

Birth of the Desire

His headphones on, Pierre — a seven-year-old I was helping with his stuttering — was frantically busy drawing one picture after another. The table and the floor were covered with the morning's work. One of the drawings immediately caught my eye. It was a nativity scene. It was nothing extraordinary for a child raised as a Roman Catholic to draw this at Christmas time. However, what had caught my attention was the composition of his picture. The creche was in the centre of the page, with baby Jesus disproportionately big, compared to the size of Mary and Joseph. It clearly was the child's space. Two curved paths wound their way in perfect symmetry from the shelter to the two lower corners of the sheet. Two stick people in the two corners, where the roads "left" the paper, were shepherds, according to Pierre. In the background above the shelter, there were two stars and two bells — two more symmetrical pairs.

I asked Pierre's mother if there were two people present when she gave birth. Surprised, she wondered how I guessed. I showed her the drawing: "Here they are, the two shepherds standing by the mother's side, while she is lying down in the birth position. The baby is still in the shelter — the womb — and the bells are Pierre's way of picturing the mother's voice."

Let me point out what was coming through Pierre's headphones. While drawing his innocent

Christmas picture, Pierre was listening to his mother's voice, which was filtered in a way that made it impossible to identify.

You are probably skeptical about my interpretation of this drawing, and with good reason. Don't children draw these kinds of things all the time?

Hearing Before Birth

André Thomas, one of the European pioneers in the field of neonatal neurology, liked to make this presentation to his students. He would first sit a newborn on a table. (In the first days of life, babies can maintain a sitting position with minimal support.) Then he would ask a few people, including the mother to stand around the table, and one by one, they would call the baby by his name. The newborn invariably leaned toward his mother.[1]

André Thomas' observation shares some common characteristics with Konrad Lorenz's well-known experiments with ducks. Lorenz regularly talked to the eggs, and when they finally hatched, the ducklings would turn their head in the direction of his voice and leave mama duck for Lorenz. You probably remember photographs of this very respectable-looking Nobel Prize winner walking the countryside escorted by a line of ducklings.

Testimonials and experimental proof of the existence

of prenatal hearing are increasing. The whole field of prenatal life has become the focus of great interest. Thomas Verny's book *The Secret Life of the Unborn Child*, published in 1981,[2] brought the notion of life before birth home to everyone... But in the early fifties, apart from the work of Dr. Lester Sontag, the field of the unborn child's reaction to sound remained unexplored territory.[3] It was only in the sixties that this kind of work started to emerge. Research in this area dealt with prenatal integration of language and ways of assessing hearing before birth.[4]

Only in the mid-sixties was it demonstrated that the eardrum, ossicles and inner ear reach adult size and become fully operational midway through pregnancy.[5] The ear completes its development well before all other sensory organs. The last missing piece to the puzzle came in 1966 when it was found that the acoustic nerve starts to myelenize — that is, it becomes able to carry a neural impulse — in the sixth month after conception. It was also discovered that most of the temporal lobe of the brain, which receives the nervous influx from the auditory nerve, is largely functional before birth.[6] In other words, not only can the ear perceive long before the child is born, but the nerve can at least partially carry the information to the brain to be processed.[7]

Testimonials and experimental proof of the existence of prenatal hearing are increasing. The whole field of prenatal life has become the focus of great interest.

THE ROOTS OF LANGUAGE

Tomatis tried to understand where language originated. He started analyzing the frequency content of the sounds emitted by an infant at the various stages of his development. On the basis of Tomatis's stipulation that the voice can emit only what the ear hears, the infant's utterances were an indication of his way of hearing. Tomatis was struck by the realization of how rapidly the control loops between the ear and the voice were being established. It was as if the system — or, at least, part of it — was already there before birth. Could that be? That prompted him to begin studying what the unborn child hears.

As early as the mid-fifties, Tomatis built an artificial womb, simulating the liquid environment, the placenta, etc. A waterproof microphone and loudspeaker were placed inside the artificial womb. The loudspeaker diffused body noises recorded from the belly of a pregnant woman who was talking during the recording. The microphone was connected to the sound analyzer. This recording would allow Tomatis to obtain the sounds the unborn infant might hear.

This analyzer indicated a sharp decrease in the low frequency sounds — such as respiration, heartbeat and other visceral noises — as if the liquid environment were filtering them out. There were also high frequency sounds present that caught Tomatis's attention, and he isolated these sounds with electronic filters. What was left, wrote Tomatis, "were barely perceptible modulations that were really 'something else.' It was this something else that interested me the most. Doubtless, it was difficult to define, and even more difficult to describe. Thus, we were confronted with the filtered sounds."[8] After an initial series of experiments, Tomatis arrived at the conclusion that these filtered sounds were the sounds of the mother's voice; thus, an unborn child could hear his mother.

THE SONIC BIRTH

Once Dr. Tomatis invited a friend to see the progress in his research on prenatal sound perception. A recording of his friend's wife was used for the demonstration. The friend brought along his young daughter. The two men were busy listening to the filtered woman's voice, while the girl was playing on her own with the headphones on. When Dr. Tomatis started to progressively unfilter the voice to show how he thought infants hear at birth, they heard the nine-year-old girl repeating to herself "'I am in a tunnel, I see two angels at the end of it, two angels in white clothes!' Then she said, 'I see Mommy.' When asked by her father how did she see her mommy, she answered, 'like this' Carried away by automatic gestures, she fell back and took up a gynecological birthing position until the tape came to an end. Then she left the laboratory, and spent the rest of the time playing, as if nothing had happened."[9] You can see where my interpretation of Pierre's drawing came from.

> The use of the filtered mother's voice is particularly effective with children who have low levels of motivation in socializing and or learning.

Tomatis shared what he had observed with child specialists and asked their opinion. For them, the little girl experienced a remembrance of her birth that had been induced by the filtered voice of her mother.

After several experiences of that kind, Tomatis started to use the filtered mother's voice with an increasing number of children. It has become a part of the passive phase of the sound stimulation program.

The use of the filtered mother's voice is particularly effective with children who have low levels of motivation in socializing and or learning. These children rapidly exhibit a greater desire to meet others and make friends. School and homework doesn't seem to be a burden anymore. Their parents often report that they tend to become more affectionate and more helpful around the house.

Children who don't talk or who tend to be oblivious to communication, such as autistic children, react very well to the filtered mother's voice. They start babbling more and then break into high-pitched screams for a few days. Then come words that they communicate with — sometimes for the first time in their life. It is as if the filtered sound of the mother's voice increases their desire to be born to a world where sound and language are a means of communication. It seems to pave the way to a development of language.

When the mother's voice is not available, the filtered music of Mozart is substituted.

LISTENING BEFORE BIRTH

In the seventies, when studying prenatal life became *the* thing to do, Tomatis's findings were challenged by the new evidence that the fetus also heard the low frequency sounds — the sounds of the mother's body. By then, having had success with the higher harmonics of the mother's voice for more than fifteen years, these findings did not make any impression on Tomatis. However, as a result of coming increasingly under fire, he decided to replicate his original experiments with more updated equipment, only to find out that the sound analyzer he had used had a defect. It systematically filtered out all sounds lower than 500 Hertz — the range of the body noises. Tomatis wrote, "as one can see, it is possible that if my initial analyzer had operated normally, I would have oriented my work around the audition of the low frequencies. And the adventure of the filtered sounds would perhaps have been ignored, or it would have been uncovered only much later."[10] Thus, we can thank a technical error for the discovery of filtered sounds.

In an effort to protect himself from the visceral noise in which he is immersed, the unborn child may attempt to "connect" with the more agreeable sound of his mother's voice.

Knowing that our ear has the ability to attune to what we want to receive and protect us from what we don't, we can appreciate that what a microphone in the uterus picks up may be different from what the fetus perceives. The defective sound analyzer operated the way listening does — as a very rudimentary zoom.

Anyone would find it unbearable to live surrounded by constant noise — such as the racket that goes on inside our body. For the sake of sanity, we would do anything to cut it off. That is what we do with the hum of the air conditioner, the gurgling of the fridge, the constant roar coming from the street — noises that are not nearly as loud as those of our body. Why should it be any different for the unborn child? In an effort to protect himself from the visceral noise in which he is immersed, the unborn child may attempt to "connect" with the more agreeable sound of his mother's voice.

Originally, Tomatis thought that the sounds of the mother's voice were perceived by the unborn child through the amniotic fluid that filtered out the low frequencies. Later he realized that as the eardrum is completely immersed in liquid, it cannot pick up or transmit any vibration. Thus, the only way the sound can reach the ear of the child-to-be-born is through bone conduction.

To hear his mother's voice by bone conduction, he puts his body against the spinal column, a column of sound. That way he is directly "plugged in" to the voice. Towards the end of pregnancy, he puts his head down against the hip bones of the mother, which become his own private auditorium at the bottom of the spine. The unborn child is now in the birth position. [11]

This body-to-body connection made by the unborn child in his quest for the mother's voice is his initial attempt to listen. Its significance is tremendous, because it is the first step toward communicating. As the mother's voice comes and goes, the very first desire is born — the desire to hear the voice — and the first gratification the pleasure of receiving it again. Repeated over and over, this desire-pleasure cycle creates a need for communication. Therefore, in the chronology of human needs, the need to reach out and to communicate seems to be the primary one, originating even before the need to be fed, which comes only after birth.[12]

> As the mother's voice comes and goes, the very first desire is born — the desire to hear the voice — and the first gratification the pleasure of receiving it again.

HEARTBEAT

It is a well-documented fact that the mother's heart-beat gives the unborn child a sense of tranquillity and of security. The repetitive, rhythmic movement of the heartbeat is picked up by the vestibular system, the ear of the body of the unborn child. It gently rocks the child day and night, bringing him a reassuring sense of continuity. This "vestibular perception" may greatly contribute to the imprint of body rhythms that pave the way for the future integration of body image, motor functions and language and for the great popularity of dance music.

• • •

Esther, a sixteen-year-old, hated her mother, she hated her father, she hated her sister, she hated men — she hated coming to the Centre. Her hatred and contempt were reflected in her appearance. She wore dirty, sloppy clothes, her hair was greasy and she was obese. Her voice was "ugly" — throaty and heavily nasal — and she was very aggressive and negative when she talked.

Her parents had separated and Esther's mother had no idea what to do with her anymore. Esther had quit school and was staying at home all day eating, feeling angry and making life miserable for everyone, including herself. When her mother asked me if Esther could be helped, I immediately thought of the filtered mother's voice and suggested a "try-and-see" program without making any promises.

"This young woman represents beauty, purity, tenderness and joy. Unfortunately the weight of the world is going to fall on her and smash her. I am this woman."

At first, Esther resisted coming to the Centre with all the might of her strong will. Her willfulness was her mother's main despair. Personally, I look at these extreme attitudes or behaviors as an expression of untapped potential. Esther was a "locomotive astray in a meadow."

At the beginning, she did not want to do a thing

while listening to the "awful scratchy noises." What she heard without recognizing it was the filtered voice of her mother. Then she started painting but destroyed everything she did. Later, the destruction was in the painting itself. She would "slash" her pictures with black paint. Later, she began to leave "windows" of color in the background of her works. However, the colors were dull, muddy, all mixed together, or had black added to them, as if to systematically remove their light — their life. This first series of paintings was very abstract.

One day, Esther drew a silhouette of a nude red woman bent over kneeling, as if worshipping. Her slim body was in a fetal position. She had drawn the woman in crayon with a surprising finesse. This drawing was a total departure from her previous works. The silhouette was in the middle of the page, encircled in a soft blue "pocket." Above her was a black vault or a cloud that looked heavy and oppressive. On the back of the picture she wrote "This young woman represents beauty, purity, tenderness and joy. Unfortunately the weight of the world is going to fall on her and smash her. I am this woman."

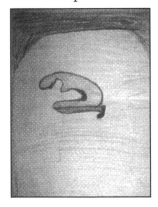

Esther continued doing abstract paintings that I could best describe as explosions of pure and vibrant colors; the muddy and black tones were gone. She then moved to colorful landscapes — Monet-like hills covered with exuberant patches of light. She painted countless flowers, which became bigger and bigger. She had to glue two, then four then eight sheets of paper together to paint just one or two of these flowers, until one day she came to the Centre with an enormous roll of paper. She even had plans of talking to the owner of the huge concrete wall right in front of the windows of the Centre to offer to decorate the wall with flowers.

The irony was that the bigger her paintings became, the more weight she was losing. She also started taking care of her appearance. She was revealing the beautiful, smart, interesting young woman that she was. Esther was still a strong-minded and opinionated woman, but these were characteristics of her personality which were to be respected. As far as I know, she continued to paint, exhibit her work and pursue a career in the arts.

I helped Esther in 1972-73 and her program lasted for about six months. I have kept a slide presentation of her drawings and I have shown them many, many times since then to illustrate what improved listening and desire to listen "look like." Esther's is a wonderful story for a clinician, one he never forgets.

• • •

The practice of the Tomatis Method requires a great deal of counselling. As a listening counselor, this perspective of the ear helped restructure my views on various aspects of life from the very beginning to the very last moments. Part II of this book is an attempt to identify the role played by listening at different times of this journey through life.

Part II — Listening Through Life

In the twenty-five years of my clinical experience, I have watched many parents complain about the difficulties they experience with their 'problem child.' While the parents are talking, I already know these difficulties hide a listening problem. Because listening is at the root of communication, a listening difficulty causes problems at home, at school, on the street.

I start wondering how many of these difficulties could have been prevented by some knowledge and understanding on the part of the parents, the teachers and the child himself. If they had known where listening is centered and "what" it does for us at the different stages of life, perhaps these problems could have been avoided. A lot can be done to respect, protect and stimulate listening from pregnancy to old age.

In this section, I will explore listening at all ages from pre-natal life and infancy to pre-schoolers and teenagers; from mid-life and working life to retirement. I also will look at children with various learning and communication problems — how to deal with these at an early stage and avoid them from reappearing in adulthood.

This section can be read by the specific chapter that corresponds to the age you're interested in understanding. However, I recommend reading the section as a whole, for an understanding of how listening unfolds from one stage of our life to another.

Birth of Listening

7

"You know, this may sound strange, but music has been a part of me since before birth," said Boris Brott — Hamilton (Ontario) Philharmonic conductor — to his radio interviewer once. "As a young man, I was mystified by this unusual ability I had to play certain pieces sight unseen. I'd be conducting a score for the first time and, suddenly, the cello line would jump out at me; I'd know the flow of the piece even before I turned the page of the score. One day, I mentioned this to my mother, who is a professional cellist. I thought she'd be intrigued because it was always the cello line that was so distinct in my mind. She was, but when she heard what the pieces were, the mystery quickly solved itself. All the scores I knew sight unseen were ones she had played while she was pregnant with me."[1]

Thomas Verny, who reports this story, mentions that other musicians such as Yehudi Menuhin and Arthur Rubinstein also claim that their musical interests could be tracked all the way to the womb. I cannot promise that you will have another Menuhin in the family, but if you want your child to develop a genuine appreciation for music, you now know when her musical education should start.

I have always found it fascinating that these musicians of the highest calibre — the best listeners on earth and those most "in touch" with their ear—know that their musical interests and talents date back to the womb.

SILENT DIALOGUE

The ear of the unborn child is bombarded by an impressive quantity of sounds — heartbeat, respiration and visceral noises of the mother's body, as well as those of her own. Amidst this continuous and repetitive noise, another kind of sound starts to emerge and take shape from time to time. This sound is clearer, more melodious. It is the mother's voice. Each time the mother-to-be uses her voice, she sends sound vibrations to the body and the ears of her unborn child who is most eager to absorb and be nourished by them.

A car radio not only provides a diversion, it also masks the noises of the car itself. We can imagine the unborn child making first attempt to "connect" with the more agreeable sound of the voice of her mother. But unlike a radio, the voice is not always "on" and the fetus cannot control it. She has to wait until it comes on to enjoy it. Thus the first motivation to reach out is born. This is followed by the first gratification — the pleasure of hearing this sound again. This initial silent "dialogue" gives birth to listening. When the voice doesn't come with any regularity, or when it is absent altogether for long periods of time, it may generate the first feelings of anxiety, or of abandonment.

> I have always found it fascinating that these musicians of the highest calibre — the best listeners on earth and those most "in touch" with their ear—know that their musical interests and talents date back to the womb.

Many mothers sense and respond to their unborn child's silent quest for dialogue. They sing the same songs over and over again. They tell stories or even engage in lively conversation with the child. But what about the quality of their voice? Does it make a difference in the way it may spark the child's desire to listen and to communicate?

We all know the difference a voice can make. A warm, friendly-sounding voice may open our mind to ideas or opinions we were not receptive to at first. It makes us listen. While we know how to say "no thanks" and close the door or hang up the phone on solicitors, we all have been caught more than once continuing to listen in spite of ourselves. Something in that voice triggered our desire to listen to it. We also may have been turned off and chased away from a showroom by nothing more than the salesman's voice and way of talking, even though we may admit that he had interesting things to say in retrospect .

The unborn child does not understand the meaning of the messages sent by the mother's voice. What he "understands" is the emotional charge of those messages. A voice that carries joy, calmness, warmth, love, hope and fulfillment is more likely to "invite" listening and the desire to communicate than a voice that carries anxiety, anger or sadness.

Expectant Father

Fathers often wonder if their own voice can have some nurturing influence on the unborn child. There is evidence that the unborn child hears her father's voice, and that this voice has a soothing affect on the newborn for the first hours of life.[2] However, the link between the father's voice and the child's ear is not nearly as direct as the mother's voice. Part of the voice sounds will be absorbed by the physical barriers before it reaches the child's ears.

I believe the greatest contribution of the expectant father is to create a warm and loving atmosphere. Because the unborn child is very much a part of her mom, everything — not just talking — the father does directly for the mother, he does directly for the child. The mother's experience of the pregnancy can be drastically changed by the father's attitude toward her and the pregnancy itself. A wonderful pregnancy for the mother means a wonderful experience for the child. All this positive energy will be transmitted to the child by the mother's warmer, richer voice.

THE MOTHER TONGUE

The mother's voice is more than an emotional nutrient and a source of vital energy for the unborn child. The rhythms and intonations specific to her voice and to the language she speaks, which is to become the child's mother tongue, impregnates her nervous system. Right from that time in life, the child "embodies" the "music of language." Psychologists and linguists, as well as parents, have always been startled by the amazing rate at which children acquire language. One of the reasons for the rapid rate of acquisition may be that it started well before birth. Henry Truby mentions that a six-month-old fetus already moves his body to the rhythm of his mother's speech.[4]

Children placed into a different language environment after birth provide vivid examples that language acquisition starts in the womb. Steven, a child adopted by an English-speaking family, came to The Listening Centre because of a history of learning disabilities. After a few days of working with Steven, it became obvious to me that his problem was primarily a motivational one — he did not want to learn. He had become a master of avoidance, making teachers and parents believe that he was not able to study. While talking to Steven's mother about his interests and hobbies, she mentioned his fascination with the French-language channels on

> The mother's voice is more than an emotional nutrient and a source of vital energy for the unborn child. The rhythms and intonations specific to her voice and to the language she speaks, which is to become the child's mother tongue, impregnates her nervous system.

TV. The mother could not understand this fascination because he had not studied French at school. At my request, the parents inquired further about Steven's birth mother, only to discover that she was French Canadian. I recommended Steven be placed in a French immersion program at school. Despite the added difficulty of the new language and of his so-called learning disability, Steven soon became more motivated and started doing well at school.

Such stories illustrate the key role of prenatal life in the acquisition of the mother tongue. The pregnant mother who lives in a bilingual or multilingual milieu should try to use the language she is most comfortable with — her mother tongue — as much as she can. A Spanish-speaking mother who lives in the U.S. and has almost no opportunity to speak Spanish, should make a point of singing, reading out loud or telling stories in Spanish during her pregnancy. This will help the child later in life to learn both Spanish and English. As we will see in the next chapter, the assimilation of other languages is possible and easy for a child once she has good mastery of her first language — her mother tongue.

Talking to the unborn child becomes critical during the fifth month of pregnancy — a time when the inner ear and its connections with the brain are operational. However, it seems very possible that the child hears even before this time. I would advise mothers to start their "daily chat" with the unborn child as soon as they know that they are expecting.

MOTHER'S MOTIONS

The ear is a receptor of movements and all movements of the mother are recorded by the unborn child. As with any other sensory stimulation, these movements have an energizing effect on the child's rapidly developing brain; they also contribute to the future development of motor functions.

Thus, walking, rocking, swimming and low impact exercises are activities that should be practiced by the mother-to-be. To facilitate the harmonization of both levels of the child's ear — the auditory and the body level — the mother should synchronize these movements with the sound of her own voice. For example, she could rock while telling stories or reciting poetry at the same time, or dancing to the sound of her own singing. Participating in natural birth exercises not only help the mother relax and prepare her for labor and delivery, they also provide both her and her child with sensory stimulation.

Listening at Birth

The ear is the sensory witness of the birth process. Sounds and movements of labor and delivery will be forever recorded. The mother's breathing, the instructions of the doctors, the sounds of pain, or excitement are all perceived by the child. The baby will also hear the very first sound she makes in this world — her first cry. At birth, the baby is suddenly exposed to an entirely different set of gravity rules. She no longer floats in the womb. Memory of these multiple sound and body experiences will often be hidden from our consciousness, but they will always remain present somewhere within ourselves. Our fears, dreams and fantasies will reflect them.

Participating in natural birth exercises not only help the mother relax and prepare her for labor and delivery, they also provide both her and her child with sensory stimulation.

The traumatic nature of birth for both the mother and the child has been described many times. While giving birth is a very natural process, it has been turned into a medical concern. With its strong lighting, medical instruments and so many strangers, the delivery room may appear to the anxious mother as a torture room.

To the criticism that hospital birth is too harsh, too violent for the mother and the newborn, the medical community's reply is that things are done this way to decrease the chances of problems. The decline in child mortality at birth these last few decades supports their point. However, a new generation of physicians, following the path set by Frederic Leboyer,[5] insists that there are other ways to help the mother with the delivery without endangering her life. Leboyer's approach respects the naturalness and the intimacy of birth for the benefit of both the mother and the child.

Through her voice, her touch, the warmth of her body, the mother can ensure a smooth transition between the world inside the womb and the new world. By being physically close to the child during the first moments of her new life, she helps the newborn experience this difficult transition without a sense of abandonment or rejection.

> Through her voice, her touch, the warmth of her body, the mother can ensure a smooth transition between the world inside the womb and the new world.

INTERRUPTED DIALOGUE

Newborn children may need to be placed in an incubator because of a health problem, or premature birth. The sad reality is that for these very reasons, they desperately need the warm, reassuring, soothing and nurturing presence of their mother.

Premature birth in particular imposes a sudden, often unexpected interruption of the mother-child dialogue. The child is cut off far too early from the sensory stimulation provided in the womb, so critical for her future motor and language development.

The incubator is sort of a sterile "bubble" that not only deprives the child of sensory stimulation, but also isolates her at the very moment she needs the physical and emotional nearness of her mother. This has become the concern of many specialists, and some incubators are now equipped with loudspeakers transmitting prerecorded heartbeat sounds to simulate the environment of the womb.

One possible way to help the newborn child

compensate for the missing sensory stimulation and the interrupted mother-child dialogue is to use recordings of the mother's voice in the incubator. This would help the child's desire to "open up," whereas lack of stimulation can make her "turn off" listening and communication altogether. The decision to open up or turn off can greatly influence the child's perception of herself, of others and of the world around her for the rest of her life. Some hospitals in Europe are now diffusing the mother's voice in incubators to create a conducive environment for the newborn.

LIFE BEFORE ADOPTION

Another interruption of the dialogue between mother and newborn that may affect her desire to listen and communicate comes when the child is given up for adoption.

Fortunately, the practice of placing newborn children in one or more foster families before finding a permanent home for them is quickly disappearing. These successive separations reinforced feelings of being abandoned and rejected, which began with the initial breakaway from the mother. These successive moves certainly were not a "welcome to life," and many youngsters and adults are still suffering from their effects.

Steps are being taken to ease the adoption process. An increasing number of newborns are adopted by their new families at the time of birth. Encounters between the natural mother and the potential adoptive parents are organized during pregnancy and the mother has a say in the choice of new parents for her child. This kind of preparation before the child is born ensures a better continuity and decreases the trauma of separation.

Despite these preventive measures, the sense of loss and of abandonment may still persist. More than 20 percent of the children who come for help at The Listening Centre are adopted. This figure is much higher than the general proportion of adopted children in the population, which does not exceed five percent.

Many of the adopted children and adolescents I have worked with shared certain characteristics, such as a sense of isolation; they also had problems with authority figures, lack of physical and emotional closeness and were ill at ease with the physical signs of affection. And almost all of the adopted people I saw had an ambivalent relationship with their adoptive mother. As children, they had usually sought her attention, but in a way that made the mother react negatively. In other words, they seemed to ask the mother to reject them over and over again. First directed toward the mother, this attitude later affected their relationship with their siblings, particularly if they were younger. If they happened to be natural children, the situation was even worse. Then, at the age of puberty, these problems at home extended to the school and in social situations.

I want to insist on the fact that I only talk about adopted youngsters that I have worked with. I know many adopted people who do not have any of these problems. At the end of a lecture on adoption, one woman was happy to tell me that she did not present any of the problems I described, even though she was adopted, while another, also adopted, said I was "right on."

There is good reason to believe that the experience of pregnancy makes a world of difference to a child's future development. Many mothers who gave their baby up for adoption enjoyed the pregnancy, welcoming the baby into life. Everything should be done to create an atmosphere around expectant mothers that is conducive to this welcome. Of all mothers-to-be, they are those who need the most and have it the least. When the father's support is absent, or when the family turns its back on the woman, it is up to us as a society — as friends and neighbours — to lend the mother a helping hand.

The Infancy of Listening

The newborn child finds himself in a new world, where sounds are transmitted through air. Listening has to overcome many challenges as the auditory system adapts to this new environment. Until this adaptation is complete, sound perception fades and the baby enters a long tunnel of auditory darkness. This may be linked with the well-known lethargy and lack of smiling observed in infants during the first two or three months of life when the ear is adapting to the new, airborne mode of auditory perception. During this period, the child risks becoming cutoff and falling into a state of sensory deprivation. What can be done to prevent or avoid this? The answer to this question may be found in an African study.

In 1958, Marcelle Gerber[1] reported that in Uganda the general development and sensory-motor learning ability of infants was months ahead of American and European children. Studying the child-rearing practices of these people, she observed that the children were generally born at home and delivered by the mother herself. They were never separated from her. The mothers slept with their babies and carried them close to their bare breasts. They continuously massaged, caressed and sang to their babies. The babies were awake a surprising proportion of the time and were alert, watchful and calm. They cried very little and smiled a lot. Both the ear and body of these infants were constantly being stimulated by the mother.

Ugandan mothers intuitively knew what we are now in the process of discovering — the importance of sensory and motor stimulation for the general well-being and development of an infant. The listening and sensory stimulation training these mothers unwittingly provided, permitted the infant to maintain a sense of continuity between life before and life after birth. It kept them in constant contact with the only part of the world they knew well — their mother — and it also prepared the path for the future integration of motor and language functions.

"ON THE MOVE"

During the first year of life, children are pulled from the realm of the horizontal to the vertical: instead of crawling, they begin to walk. At that time they develop a multitude of functions at an amazingly rapid pace. The brain requires a huge quantity of stimulation to respond to all these needs. All this is orchestrated by the ear of the body, which also provides the child with the energy necessary to see this development to completion.

Children amaze adults with their capacity to be relentlessly "on the move." An adult trying to imitate all the movements of an infant would be exhausted in less than two hours. It is important for children to be placed in an environment that encourages them to move around. A baby left in his crib for most of the day does not have enough opportunity to stimulate his brain, which may delay or impair his motor development. Children who stay in an incubator for an extended period of time are even more likely to exhibit a slower motor development.

Touching the child and playfully tossing and turning him add to the sensory stimulation that feeds the brain and thus helps in the growth of both mind and body. Talking and singing to the infant while holding him allows a body-to-body transmission of the sound — through vibration of the bone structure — which was the pre-natal way of perceiving the mother's voice. It strengthens the link between life before and after birth.

In many cultures, the mother carries the child on her back. The child's body clings to the mother's spinal column, allowing him to receive the mother's voice by bone conduction. In Western cultures, we push our babies in strollers or baskets, depriving them of this direct and enriched contact with sounds.

THE TALKING EAR

Language acquisition soon follows the development of motor function. If all goes well, they continue to evolve in tandem, indicating that the ear of the body and the auditory ear are working in harmony. Through movements and sounds, the child explores himself and the world around him. This exploration in sound will become language.

The process starts when children hear the sounds they inadvertently produce when they laugh and cry. Then comes the game of listening to themselves playing over and over with the sound of their voice.

Children with normal hearing are quick to realize that they can change at will the sounds with which they are playing. Sounds coming from other sources can also be imitated — the roar of the engine, the tick-tock of the clock, the bark of the dog, the "choo-choo" of the train, the words of people around them.... It is later that children

discover that the sounds they are playing with provoke a reaction from others. "Mom" brings their mother close. The meaning hidden in the word starts to
unfold. The sounding game becomes a means to communicate. Speech is born!

Because their auditory system fails to respond and
control these first involuntary sounds, deaf children
don't progress from this stage or may soon stop making
these sounds. The sounding game does not occur with
these children, thus causing mutism.

Remember that a few days after birth, the newborn
was forced into an auditory tunnel. How and when
does he get out of it? As the middle ear progressively
adapts to the new acoustic environment, the auditory
spectrum opens and the infant is able to perceive, emit
and imitate a wider and wider range of sounds. Regardless of what the mother tongue is, they will be sounds
such as *Ma*, *Da*, *Do*, *Po*, etc. These first phonemes pronounced by the child have a low frequency content. This
tends to indicate that auditory reopening starts with
the ability to listen in the low frequency range. We have
all heard young children sing charmingly out of tune.
They do so because they are still unable to control the
higher range of their voice.

Like a fan, this listening ability progressively
unfolds, to include the medium and then the high frequency sounds. The last phonemes to be fully controlled
by the child are those containing sibilants — sounds
richest in higher harmonics. Sibilant phonemes in the
English language are *ch*, *s*, *z*, *f*, and *th*. Many children
still lisp at the age of three, four or even five. This may
mean that their auditory "fan" has not yet completely
unfolded. That may also be why most phonetic spelling
mistakes affect those same sibilant sounds.

Body Listening and Body Language

Oral language, like music, has its own rhythm, its own
movement, which is associated with the low frequency

range of the sound spectrum. The vestibular ear — integrator of all body movements — is therefore fully involved in speech production. Before printing was invented, oral tradition was the way of passing down knowledge from one generation to another. Texts were composed in verses and were repeated as incantations while people walked. (It is not surprising that in poetry the unit used to measure rhythm is called a "foot.") This oral tradition involved both levels of the ear — the body and the auditory. Such a style of learning allowed for an astounding memory capacity — the very memory the child needs to successfully acquire language.

From a very early age, we begin to perceive and respond to the rhythm of language. This rhythm component accounts for what is to become intonation, inflections of the voice and the gestures that accompany talking — all part of verbal expression.

Researchers from Boston University have used video technology to study the so-called involuntary movements of newborn babies and found out that body movements of the infants were synchronized with the language sounds they heard.[2] These body responses were so consistent that they could be catalogued. In the previous chapter we saw that body responses to mother's speech are already present before birth.

Singing nursery rhymes to the baby, while rocking him, gives a chance for his body and his auditory ear to work in harmony. It allows the child to embody the rhythm of "the music of language." His memory, his oral expression, and, later on, his written language will all benefit from this early pastime.

Later on, telling or reading poems to the child will also have that harmonizing effect; poetry amplifies the music of language. Unfortunately, many children are never exposed to poetry. Most of us first encounter poetry as part of the school curriculum. In this artificial setting, it loses its freshness and spontaneity. One may quickly conclude that it is something old-fashioned, somewhat ridiculous and boring.

As soon as children discover they can control the sounds coming out of their mouths, they start playing with their voices. As I mentioned before, the sounding game comes first, and the meaning follows. Children can repeat the same words and sentences over and over again, completely out of context and with no intent of using them to communicate. Children make up their own "private speech"[3] — a "magical language" — to paraphrase Piaget, who coined the term "magical thinking," and Pearce, who entitled his book *The Magical Child*.[4] This magical language is the first poetry children ever compose. Parents who worry about such behavior and wonder if it is aberrant should relax. There are some famous precedents of this kind of language. Before going to bed every night, baby Mozart would sing a tune of his own invention with funny words like"Oragna figata fa, marina gamina fa."[5] This sounding game is an exercise that "attunes" the ear, the body, the nervous system and the voice, until the production of such an intricate series of complex sounds becomes automatic and spontaneous. This attuning is similar to a musician practicing his scales over and over again, to fully master the musical phrase. For children, it is a listening game to master the control of speech.

Controlled voice production for speech is a highly complex phenomenon. To understand its complexity, we have to remember that what is called the phonatory apparatus consists of muscles, organs or body cavities whose functions are unrelated to speaking. The mouth, lips and tongue have the intake of food as their primary function. The lungs, nasal cavities and pharynx are part of the respiratory system. The larynx is a sort of valve that prevents us from swallowing and breathing in air at the same time. Many animals have all this at their disposal, but having an apparatus doesn't lead to speech. It is the active interplay between the voice, the listening ear and nervous system, which takes control of each of these individual elements and "orchestrates" them for an entirely new and different use: the production of speech. To do so, involvement of both levels of the ear, the one that provides acoustic models of language sounds and the other that monitors the shaping of all the body elements implicated in the production of these sounds, is required. As musicians play the scales with their instruments, children have to use their body to play the scales of language. The body becomes the "language instrument."

> As musicians play the scales with their instruments, children have to use their body to play the scales of language. The body becomes the "language instrument."

Speech requires a use of the language instrument at an extraordinarily fast rate. To speak North American English it is necessary to produce an average of thirteen phonemes, thirteen "notes," per second! So let children talk to themselves, let them make up words for the songs they sing, tell silly stories or produce all kinds of weird sounds. There is no such thing as knowing too many nursery rhymes. Even though they may seem pointless or seem to have little meaning, their phonetic content is quite rich and they go a long way in shaping a child's listening. The same holds true for children's poetry and stories, which should have both a lively rhythmic content, as well as a colourful phonetic one.

BILINGUAL LISTENING

Young children exposed to new languages attune their language instrument in the same way.

Christine was a five-year-old French girl who spent her holidays in southern Spain. All day long she played with Spanish children and her total lack of Spanish didn't seem to bother her in the least. In the evenings, her parents, who didn't speak a word of Spanish, were amazed to hear her talking to herself in fluent Spanish. In fact, it was not Spanish at all — she was making up a language which sounded like Spanish but had no meaning whatsoever. Gradually, however, this make-believe language started to include real Spanish words, and then phrases. Christine would still talk to herself or pretend she was carrying on a conversation with her parents in Spanish. At the end of the month, she could communicate and even argue with her new friends. She spoke real Spanish! I have had the opportunity to observe the same phenomenon over and over again with children in the different countries where I have lived and worked.

We can all learn a lot from the way children acquire a new language. Christine intuitively knew that to assimilate a foreign language one must start to assimilate the "music" of this language first; the meaning follows automatically. The implication of such a "listening" way to learn is tremendous for the teaching of foreign languages, and also for the teaching of reading, which will be discussed in later chapters.

Younger children are able to learn two or more languages at a time if they are exposed to native speakers of this language. I insist on this point because in numerous situations when families live in a foreign country, the parents feel that they have to speak to the child in the language of that country. They want to help the child become part of his new milieu. Very often, they also do it under pressure from school: teachers tell them that the child must speak the new language at home in order to do better at school. Unfortunately, in most situations, the parents speak the language with an accent. What happens then? The child gets used to it and the language is assimilated with that accent. To draw a comparison with music, it is like learning to sing the lyrics of one song to the melody and rhythm of another.

Gloria has learned English from her Mexican

parents, who both speak English with a strong Spanish accent. She knows English but she perceives it as a Mexican person would. When she is at school, she hears her English teacher speaking English with a strong English accent and she is lost. Imagine how much of what the teacher is saying is lost to Gloria, while she is busy "translating" the teacher's accent. Once the teacher's accent is translated, she still has to make up for the information she missed. She becomes frustrated and her work suffers. The alarmed teacher asks the parents to help Gloria with her homework, because she is not following in class. However, the "help" the parents offer Gloria in their Spanish-sounding English does no good at all.

> Younger children are able to learn two or more languages at a time if they are exposed to native speakers of this language.

An even worse situation arises if the specific listening channels of the two languages get mixed up. As a result, the child may start to speak a mixture of both languages. I have known some children who were so unintelligible that even the parents didn't understand what they were saying. The reality in those cases is that neither of the two languages has been learned. The child has developed a listening problem, and a learning disability is likely to appear in the early grades at school. With such confusion, it is no wonder that these children have problems learning to read, write and spell.

Another special situation that requires careful handling can occur when the two parents have different mother tongues and speak the new language with a strong accent. In this case, no matter what language the parents use to talk to each other, each parent should address the child in his or her own language, even if this means that the child has to learn a third language for school. If Mom is French, Dad is German and the family lives in the U.S., children will speak French with Mom, German with Dad and English at school and on the street. Remember, if a child is young enough, he can develop as many listening channels as are necessary.

The best thing the parents can do to prepare their children for the acquisition of a new language is to find playmates for them who are fluent in that language. Usually, that's all the children need. Spontaneous learning — that is, learning without being aware of it — is the best way to acquire a language. It is true for adults, as well as children. However, unlike children, adults are often so self-conscious when learning a new language that all spontaneity vanishes. And what can the French parents do when the teacher says that Jean's English is not good enough for grade one? Send him to play with the English neighbour even more often and trust him! Not being ready "yet" is much better than being confused.

The school system should also be aware of these basic guidelines. Teachers and social workers who work in multicultural communities or in areas with a high proportion of immigrants are often in the best position to advise parents on such matters. The U.S. has to deal with an increasing number of Spanish-speaking immigrants. A good and peaceful assimilation begins with the breaking of the language barrier. This starts as early as nursery school and it has to begin with the understanding that a child can become perfectly bilingual. We have to be careful not to "mix the channels" and end up with a child who has to deal with not one, but with two language barriers. Such a child will be uncomfortable in both communities.

WHEN THE EAR GETS FLOODED

Otitis Media, more widely known as ear infection, is the most common illness among children. It may have devastating effects on listening even after hearing is fully restored. The Eustachian tube closes as a result of allergies, cold or other infections, thus causing a vacuum and eventual fluid build-up in the middle ear cavity.[6]

Interestingly, the time in life when children are most prone to ear infections is when they need their listening the most — during the phase of language acquisition. As we learned before, this acquisition is the direct consequence of the opening up of the child's sensory system — and of his ears in particular. This is the time when the child uses his listening to reach out, to build a bridge to the outside world by means of language. But, if for one reason or another, the opening up is no longer welcome, a "flooding" of the ears may well be one of the possible ways to stop listening. Could one think of a more radical way to stop listening than to close up the ears? While an ear infection is an obvious physical illness most often associated with colds or allergies, in some cases it has a psychological cause. My years of clinical practice have shown me that a higher incidence of ear infections is found during difficult times in the child's life: a sibling's birth, a separation from home or an early entry into nursery school, or at times of tension in the family.

Whatever their cause, ear infections elicit a temporary drop in the hearing level which may impair the mechanism of listening. When the middle ear is flooded, the ear drum, the ossicles and the "listening muscles" cannot operate properly. As the infection progresses, this fluid, which at first has the consistency of water, becomes as thick and sticky as glue, making it more and more difficult for the ear to operate properly. The resulting middle ear disruption may continue to affect listening well after the infection is over.

> At the time of language acquisition, when every day counts, ear infections may weaken listening for weeks, months and even years.

At the time of language acquisition, when every day counts, ear infections may weaken listening for weeks, months and even years. More than 56 percent of children with learning disabilities that we see at The Listening Centre have had a history of ear infections.[7] In my opinion, the ear infection is the single greatest cause of learning disabilities and attentional deficit disorders. This is to say that it is critical to find ways to prevent or, if that is not possible, to treat the infection as rapidly as possible.

The earliest preventive measure is for the mother to breastfeed her child. Research has consistently shown decreased incidence of ear infections in children who have been breast-fed. If bottle-fed, the child should not be put to bed with a bottle, as the liquid could find its way to the middle ear and flood it when the child is asleep.

When a child is prone to repeated ear infections, he should probably be tested for allergies. Milk and milk products, as well as products with a high content of acidity, such as canned orange juice, tend to increase mucus production. A reduction or total removal of these products from the diet may decrease the risk of ear infections. Family physicians, allergists, homeopaths and naturopaths can provide excellent insights into all potential causes of allergic reactions.

Ear infections are easy to detect because they are most often painful. However, there are exceptions. Very young children may feel and express the pain, but be unable to pinpoint its source, whereas other children may simply not feel the pain. In those cases, it is necessary to know some of the secondary effects of the infection. The first and most common one is partial loss of hearing. Older children may ask others to repeat what they have said or just not respond. Their speech may become unclear, poorly articulated and difficult to understand. They may also be more clinging, moody and cranky for no apparent reason. Whereas some children may become more hyper, others may become more apathetic. Their sleeping may be disturbed, making them unusually tired and pale in the morning. The ear of the body may also send out signals such as clumsiness, poor coordination and poor body posture. The sick child's temperature may rise, and he may tend to rub and pull on his ears. When some of these signs appear for no apparent reason, it is time to go to the doctor to have the ears checked.

Listening for Preschoolers

School brings yet new challenges for listening. So far learning has been spontaneous, led by the child's desire to discover the world. At school it will be learning for learning's sake. Children will be required to sit still and to keep quiet, to stop using their bodies and voices. This is unfortunate as the most efficient way of stimulating their ears and nervous system is by using their bodies and voices. What a contrast between this new situation that adults call "work" and the "play" situation that children know so well and enjoy so much!

Schoolwork may quickly become synonymous with "hard," or "boring." Unfortunately, the word "listen" — as in "listen now" or "listen to me" — may also become associated with school and work. When the body is not receiving enough stimulation, listening is not sustained for long, and the child needs to be reminded to tune in. Listening, which should be automatic and spontaneous, begins to signify effort and becomes allied with the notion of discipline. This unfortunate association may never disappear completely.

As for play, it will have to wait until recess, after-school, weekends and vacations. Playing is easy and fun, and has an aura of freedom and permissiveness. Even highly structured and disciplined, sports are viewed as play. They are fun and therefore few kids are late for a hockey practice.

At the time when computers were not yet widely used in the school system, I observed that many children who did poorly in math and found it boring did similar exercises well on the home computer. Math meant school and work; the computer meant games, play, fun. This "fun" image of the computer is rapidly changing with its introduction into the schools.

> Nursery school and kindergarten are the time when the child's listening is most flexible. This is when the child learns the fastest and with the most success; it is prime learning time — provided the child maintains a high level of motivation.

When a child is led by her desire to win in sports, or to use the computer, she finds the structure and discipline necessary to reach her goal within herself. In a play situation, motivation leads to action, which in turn leads to success, exploration and discovery. When a child encounters an obstacle in the play situation, she goes out of her way to find a solution.

How can we help children to maintain their "built-in" spontaneous way of learning? How can we get them to perceive work as synonymous with play? In other words, how can we keep their listening stimulated at school? These questions should be addressed in preschool, before the children are taught to sit still and keep quiet, before teaching becomes academic and formal.

Nursery school and kindergarten are the time when the child's listening is most flexible. This is when the child learns the fastest and with the most success; it is prime learning time — provided the child maintains a high level of motivation. The way the child experiences her first introduction to school greatly affects her attitude toward it and therefore her motivation to learn for years to come.

GOODBYE HOME

The child is often sent to nursery school when the mother either wishes or has to return to work. Depending on how it is presented to her, the child may experience nursery school as a place where she is dropped because Mom and Dad have no time for her. School may come to mean not only separation, but also abandonment, rejection. The worst situation — a common one among children with learning problems — is one in which a child is placed in a nursery school at the time of the birth of a sibling. This child is likely to have a strong negative reaction to school because of its associations.

The first school day should be an exciting event — and it easily can be if parents prepare the child months in advance for the idea of going to school. School is the place where one goes to play and make a lot of new friends. The child could meet some of her future schoolmates before actually beginning school. Parents could take the child to the school a few times beforehand to meet the teacher and the children and to get acquainted with the classroom atmosphere. Once prepared for it, the prospect of going to school becomes an enticing one.

A child who tends to be upset when separated from her mother could be brought to school the first few days by the father or any other adult. However, the child should not be withdrawn from school if the child cries or acts difficult at the beginning. If she realizes that her behaviour can influence her parents and teachers, she will surely take advantage of it and become truly difficult.

Training the preschool child's listening requires a strong emphasis on activities such as listening to music, singing, talking, reciting, acting — activities which combine the use of sounds with body movements.

Nursery rhymes, which are easy to sing in a group, are the most appropriate pieces of music to use. Children are more attuned to the voices of other children than to adults' voices. Thus they will respond better to nursery rhymes sung by kids. Preschool is also the place where children can be introduced to classical music. It can be used as background music for some kind of quiet individual activity, such as drawing or coloring. The music of Mozart induces movement of the hand, and much artwork done while listening to it looks like waves. These waves on paper — the graphic expression of a dance of the hand — are an invitation for the gestures of the future cursive writing. Both relaxing and energizing, the music of Mozart can be used either to calm down the children when they are restless, "hyper" or fidgety, or to give them a boost when they are tired or distractable. Baroque music can also be used in those situations.

> Training the preschool child's listening requires a strong emphasis on activities such as listening to music, singing, talking, reciting, acting — activities which combine the use of sounds with body movements.

The sound system used in the classroom should be of good quality and kept well maintained. Children's listening is to a great extent shaped by the sounds to which they are exposed. Their listening is extremely malleable and it does not take much to induce auditory distortion and confusion.

Singing

Singing is one of the most beautiful talents we possess. It relieves the pressure when our feelings and emotions get too intense. It is the most efficient way to "charge our batteries." It is also a means of communication that goes beyond language. It is not a coincidence that all religions have their own songs and sacred chants. There are military songs, scout songs, school songs, and so on. Each country has its national anthem, and some corporations even have their own flagship song.

But how many of us sing? We did sing earlier on, long ago, but something happened and we stopped. We could have been discouraged, or maybe we were laughed at. For one reason or another, we became self-conscious and stopped singing. Let's not reproduce history. Let's let our children sing!

Once again, preschool is a perfect setting for singing provided two conditions are fulfilled. First, the teacher must enjoy singing and not be inhibited if she does not have the greatest voice. However, if it is really that bad, something can be done to improve it (see Earobic Exercise, Part III). Second, children should sing in their natural voices and it doesn't matter if the voice is off pitch. What matters is that the children enjoy singing and that the more they sing, the more they want to sing.

A good time to sing at school is early in the morning. It opens the ears and the mind, clears up the voice and sets the mood for the rest of the day.

PLAYING MUSIC

Playing a musical instrument is another possible preschool listening activity. It harmonizes auditory and body control and by doing so prepares the path for reading and writing. However, a child who doesn't show any inclination to play an instrument should not be forced to do so. Children should be invited to choose which musical instrument they want to play. One should not impose piano, just because there is a piano at Grandma's. Each musical instrument has a specific sound range, and children tend to choose the instrument that most suits their own. Forcing a child to play a certain instrument is like making someone sing soprano without any consideration of her own vocal register. To make a choice, the child needs to hear, see, touch, blow or strum different instruments.

TALKING

Clear and structured verbal expression is one of the keys for clear and well-structured thinking.

When done in a rich and well-articulated voice, the simple act of talking exercises listening skills. Making children speak well is one of the most radical ways to train their listening. This doesn't mean that every pre-school teacher should become a speech therapist. Children like acting and reciting poems, and learning a new language is easy for them. The teacher should take advantage of the children's listening, as well as their imaginativeness, spontaneity and playfulness.

In acting, having to imitate someone else's voice automatically makes children work on their elocution. It makes them listen to themselves and, by doing so, forces them to control their voice and body movements while talking.

Children usually like to act, but some are more at ease with expressing themselves through someone else. They make their dolls answer for them and make the dolls talk to each other. Acting by improvisation has the added advantage of letting out the emotions that the children would not otherwise be able to express. It also lets their imagination and creativity loose. Puppets or, better yet, puppets created by the children themselves offer an ideal medium for spontaneous acting.

Reciting poetry is another way to enrich a child's voice, particularly her intonation. It will also increase her vocabulary and train her memory. I am aware that reciting poetry is a rare practice in North America and that many educators

In acting, having to imitate someone else's voice automaticaly makes children work on their elocution. It makes them listen to themselves and, by doing so, forces them to control their voice and body movements while talking.

view it as an old-fashioned teaching technique that would bore "modern" children to death. But children like poetry, when it is presented to them for what it is — a music made of words. We remember that children have been composing their own kind of private poetry ever since they uttered their first sounds. They relate to it perfectly.

Poetry is like singing. To make it "sing" even more, a melody can be added. Putting poetry to music makes it easier to memorize and adds to its playfulness.[1]

WELCOMING A NEW LANGUAGE

Not only is bilingualism an undisputable "mind-opener," it also provides a fabulous way to expand the child's listening. In social interactions, propelled by his desire to communicate, the child spontaneously acquires a broad range of vocabulary and the complex structures to make up meaningful sentences. He automatically learns to speak. Unfortunately, when the child learns a second language in a classroom, this spontaneous learning is often replaced by rote memorization of lists of words, regular and irregular verb conjugations, rules of grammar, exceptions to those rules and so on. This is a far cry from the unforced learning of the mother tongue — at school, the child has to "work" his way to knowledge. For children to excel at learning a new language, it has to be as much fun and as spontaneous and apparently effortless as learning their mother tongue was.

> For children to excel at learning a new language, it has to be as much fun and as spontaneous and apparently effortless as learning their mother tongue was.

To become bilingual, the child doesn't necessarily have to live in a bilingual family. However, he needs to be exposed to the new language before the age of six. This makes preschool the prime time for this exposure. The child could be placed in a language immersion pre-school, where the new language is the mother tongue of the teachers. Being part of a group of children who are fluent in that particular language would provide a perfect setting for spontaneous learning. If the parents are not fluent in that language, they should try to avoid using it with the child — just remember Gloria's confusion.

It will soon be time for the child to enter primary most difficult hurdles his listening will ever encounter.

Listening at School

ohnny has turned six, and the big day has arrived. He has to leave the house today just a little earlier than usual in the morning — he is now a proud grade one student!

School brings with it an atmosphere very different from that of kindergarten. The academic mode of teaching, the one that Johnny now has to get used to, is geared to those who are comfortable with logic and abstract reasoning.

Kindergarten teachers have commented that Johnny does best in a hands-on situation; he has a more experiential, action-oriented learning style and is somewhat uncomfortable when it comes to putting his thoughts into words. The teachers have also observed that it has taken Johnny a long time to learn numbers and the letters of the alphabet. Many children will compensate for their auditory and language weaknesses by using visual and tactile support. For instance, children's books are replete with illustrations, and kids like Johnny learn to interpret the pictures rather than actually reading the letters — and their visual interpretations can be amazingly accurate. They may use their fingers and visualize all sorts of objects to help them count. But even though some children become masters at this, there are only so many portions a pie can be divided into — and so many fingers to count on.

As numbers grow in digits and the illustrations disappear from books, this very concrete way of problem-solving has to be replaced by a more abstract one. The student is confronted with an auditory mode of learning. This transition, which already began in kindergarten, is completed between grades three and five. Listening skills prepare and enable the child to master this new kind of learning.

My intention is not to propose another teaching technique, nor is it to suggest that the existing system should be changed. Rather, it is to show parents and teachers what can be done to help children use all the dimensions of their listening for learning within their school system. I have provided a checklist in Appendix B that you can use to assess your child's listening.

Sustaining children's motivation to learn while introducing the academic material is the first challenge of a primary school teacher. The successful teacher is the one who can blend the action-oriented and playful atmosphere of the kindergarten into the more formal school structure. Johnny and most other children will thrive if allowed to learn spontaneously.

> My intention is not to propose another teaching technique, nor is it to suggest that the existing system should be changed. Rather, it is to show parents and teachers what can be done to help children use all the dimensions of their listening for learning *within* their school system.

Teaching material can be presented as a new and exciting world to be discovered. A newcomer in a city quickly learns to identify the town hall, the commercial centers, the churches, a few restaurants, but he doesn't yet know how to get from one to another. He needs a map. The newcomer to a primary school has a lot of information, but he doesn't yet know how it all fits together. The teacher is there to give him a map of knowledge, that is, a structure, guidelines, points of reference and a general direction. Why not present each subject as a story with a beginning and an end, made up of episodes; each lesson can be a new episode in the story. Easily applicable for something like history and geography, it can also be applied to math and languages.

The complaint most often heard from teachers of children with learning disabilities is that they have a short attention span. Attention Deficit Disorder — ADD — is becoming a household word of the nineties. This deficit may manifest itself in many ways — distractibility, day dreaming, poor concentration, fidgety behaviour and hyperactivity.

> Attention span is the ability to listen (well) for a prolonged period of time; it is "listening plus a time factor." You can imagine how important that ability is during the long classroom hours. The best way I know of improving attention span is to work on listening.

Years of work with children have led me to conclude that attention span is the ability to listen (well) for a prolonged period of time; it is "listening plus a time factor." You can imagine how important that ability is during the long classroom hours. The best way I know of improving attention span is to work on listening.[1]

Concentration, on the other hand, is the ability to cut out parasitic information in order to "listen to oneself thinking." Concentration, at least at a young age, can be viewed as "listening to one's thoughts" — a certain listening of the mind. Some children give a good illustration of how concentration works. When asked a question, they say, "Let me think." Then they retreat into themselves — often closing their eyes — in a sort of inner conversation, as if they had to listen to the answer coming from inside.

To help children maximize their attention span at school is to help them maximize their listening. We can do this by keeping their desire to learn burning, providing plenty of sensory stimulation, starting with that of the teacher's voice, and reducing the "parasite" background noises.

THE VOICE OF KNOWLEDGE

Keeping students' listening stimulated largely depends on the quality of the teacher's voice. There are voices that wake us up and voices that put us to sleep — those that catch our attention and those that put us off listening. The teacher should always keep in mind that her voice supplies not only the knowledge, but also the very energy that permits that knowledge to sink in and be recorded.

For instance, Dad says that when he talks about baseball, Johnny can keep his attention "on" indefinitely. On the other hand, Johnny's teacher says that he has a short attention span. "Why is it that he listens well at home and not at school? Is Johnny lazy?" Dad asks. Wait, let's not jump to conclusions. When it comes to baseball, Johnny knows everything: the teams, the players' names, the rules…. At school, most of what the teacher talks about is new — the names, the terminology, the rules. Johnny needs a lot more energy and time to absorb and understand all this new information. And he needs all the help he can get.

The teacher's voice is especially important in helping children become better listeners; it provides a necessary rhythm and energy. A well-articulated voice is rich in timbre — in high frequency "charging" sounds — and will stimulate listening and keep the mind awake. The message will sound so much clearer, that it will be processed more easily. Good articulation also slows down the rate of speech, giving more time for the information to be absorbed. Slowing down gives the teacher a chance to vary her intonation and to be more expressive. It also allows time for her body to become an active part of speaking. This will in turn involve her student's ear of the body in the act of listening.

> The teacher should always keep in mind that her voice supplies not only the knowledge, but also the very energy that permits that knowledge to sink in and be recorded.

If you are a teacher, there are numerous ways to assess the quality and impact of your voice. A video is a good way to see yourself from your students' perspective. You can also compare your level of energy at the beginning of the school day with that at the end. If you have a good voice, you will likely feel much more energetic after school is over and so will your students. If you don't have a good voice, all is not lost: the Earobics exercises in Part III of the book will help.

LISTENING BREAKS

Just as rest areas are necessary along highways for drivers, rest times are also necessary during classes for students and their listening. These rest times may take the form of a stretch, deep breath, free conversation between the students for a few minutes, discussion on the topic of the day, etc. Talking stimulates listening, and letting students talk has an added benefit of letting them "recharge their batteries." A good laugh from time to time also provides an excellent "stretch." Rest time should be planned every fifteen to twenty minutes. When the subject is particularly demanding, such as an introduction of a new math concept, the time between breaks can be reduced. This helps reduce the negative impact that "sitting still and keeping quiet" has on listening.

Washing, brushing his teeth, getting dressed, having breakfast are all part of a child's morning routine. And what about his listening maintenance? Does he sing in the shower or listen to some lively music before going to school? The reading aloud exercise, described in Part III, can give a day a wonderful boost if practiced for about ten minutes every morning. To kill two birds with one stone, the study material could be reviewed out loud. And to add another bird, if done before and during homework, this exercise also enhances concentration. (See Earobic Exercise 10, Part III).

PARASITES OF LISTENING

Good listeners block out background noise to tune in exclusively to the teacher's voice. But not all students are good listeners. Reducing background noise and other parasitic information benefits everyone — good listeners included. What can be done to make the space of a classroom more conducive to listening?

Distractible, fidgety and scattered students will do best in the front row, with mostly their right ear exposed to the teacher's voice.

Most incidental classroom noises are feet shuf-

Good listeners block out background noise to tune in exclusively to the teacher's voice. But not all students are good listeners. Reducing background noise and other parasitic information benefits everyone — good listeners included.

fling and chairs scratching the floor. To decrease these sounds, the floor of the classroom could be covered with padded vinyl. However, it would not do to use materials such as acoustic tiles on the ceiling or sound absorbing material on the walls; these materials absorb the high frequency, "charging portion" of all sounds and they create a "dead" atmosphere, certainly not conducive to listening. We want a classroom to be a lively space. It should provide a genuine invitation for listening.

It is not just the auditory ear that listens at school. The ear of the body does as well. To take both these levels into account, a "listening posture" should be encouraged. (See Earobic Exercise 1, Part III.) To stimulate both levels of his listening ear, Johnny should be sitting up straight with his feet firmly planted on the floor — if available an adjustable height chair with a straight back is best.

Still very much in the context of sensory stimulation, although not directly related to listening, fluorescent lighting is known to provoke fatigue, affecting attention span and concentration. A hyperactive child tends to be more fidgety when exposed to this kind of light and a distractable child daydreams even more. Many architects have become aware of the highly negative effects of fluorescent lighting and avoid using it.

Children with a Lot of "Hype"

As we have seen, attention span and concentration are very much related to listening. Certain types of hyperactivity can be viewed as an attentional problem at both the auditory and the body level of listening — the two ends of the antenna. But even in these cases, listening is only one of many factors involved.

Contrary to appearances, a hyperactive child is not one with too much energy; rather he is a child who has poor control of his energy. Like other children, he is constantly stimulated by sensory information. What is different in his case is that this energy is not channeled properly; it is lost throughout the body and mind. An end result of this energy loss is that the child gets tired easily — he may tend to fall asleep quickly — and shows various attentional deficits. I have observed that with some children, the energy loss becomes more obvious at puberty, when certain signs of hyperactivity disappear or are better controlled. The inability to focus, distractibility and a tendency to get tired are still evident — sometimes combined with a new apathetic behavior. An "ex-hyperactive" adolescent once told me, "They think I am not hyper anymore, but I know that my mind still is."

> Certain types of hyperactivity can be viewed as an attentional problem at both the auditory and the body level of listening — the two ends of the antenna.

Like the terms "learning disability," "minimal brain dysfunction," "emotional disturbance," the term "hyperactivity" is a catchall that is used too loosely. From the point of view of listening, at least two main types of hyperactive children stand out, as we shall see when we look at Bradley and Sandy.

Bradley has the reputation of being a trouble-maker — he somehow gets involved in all sorts of fights; he has problems with his teachers, his friends and his family. To top it off, his grades have been getting progressively worse. And everybody agrees that at times he can be the most agreeable and considerate kid, and one of the best students. Brad's Listening Test shows weak responses in the low frequency range — an indication that he is not in touch with his ear of the body. However, he is most sensitive to the high frequency charging sounds. One end of the antenna is not doing enough while the other is working overtime, thus creating an imbalance. Brad's tremendous amount of energy cannot be properly channeled. As a result, a lot of "short-circuiting potential" is spilling over into aggravation. To put it yet another way, Brad has a powerful motor but unreliable steering and brakes.

Sandy is a passive, absentminded, highly distractable young girl with hardly any spark in her eyes. Her hands are jellylike, as if they had no bones. She has been described by some specialists as hyperactive because of her attentional deficit and her tendency to fidget constantly. Other than this, she has nothing in common with Bradley except for poor marks — the term "hypo-activity" may be more appropriate for her. Sandy's Listening Test is also quite different from Brad's. It indicates weaknesses and distortions in the high frequency range, meaning that she misses most of the "charging" sounds. Moreover, she is too sensitive to low frequency sounds, such as the hum of the air conditioning, feet shuffling in the classroom and other disturbing background noises.

Not all children who are difficult and exhibit impulsive behaviour are hyperactive children. Many of them are simply reacting to stressful situations in the family or to pressure at school by being difficult. It is their way of releasing stress. Playing with the word, I would call these children "hyperreactive."

In most situations of "hyperactivity," family counselling is the answer. When the child "hyperreacts" at school, it may be wise to review how appropriate the particular school is. The "acting up" of many hyperreactive children is due to their inability to speak out because of a listening problem.

For children with hyperactivity, I highly recommend activities that help channel physical energy, such as exercise. They all lead to better body control, which is lacking in a lot of these children. Martial arts also provide a means to help the child control his impulsive and aggressive tendencies, tendencies that are fairly common among hyperactive children. This works on the ear of the body.

Hyperactive children often give the impression that they act first and think later — when it is too late. It is interesting to note that, as with many children who have language and learning problems, hyperactive children seldom use, or have used, a private language when they were younger. This suggests that they did not and probably still do not listen to themselves. To establish this "listening loop," I recommend to these children that they record short tapes in their mind.

Brian would kick his classmates and shout at them if they did something he didn't like. This behavior had already gotten him in trouble at school several times and had given him the reputation of a class disturber. He hated having this reputation and reacted the only way he knew how — by shouting and kicking. This, of course, got him into even more trouble. Worst of all, he wound up having no friends. I asked Brian to memorize the sentence: "Kicking and fighting means trouble — don't." I then told him to repeat the sentence out loud several times, then close his eyes and say it to himself silently. Then to open his eyes and listen to his voice repeat the sentence in his mind. I then asked him to repeat the sentence each time he was about to attack one of the other kids. It didn't take long before a beaming Brian was telling me about the new friends he had made at school, and the teacher was commenting about a tremendous change in Brian's attitude. Several different "tapes" can be recorded like this, to be used in various situations as they come up. To be effective, each mental recording should be short and to the point: "Wait for my turn." "Put my hand up before I speak" or "Walk, don't run." This trick is worth trying as it often works.

I cannot talk about children with short attention spans and hyperactive children without mentioning the two definite things to avoid — TV and junk food. Long exposure to TV makes these children more irritable. There are several problems associated with TV. One is the continuous low frequency buzzing sound generated by most TV sets. This background noise produces tiredness, as does the fluorescent TV screen.

Another problem is that the sound quality of many TV sets are of inferior quality. Not only does that have a detrimental effect on the ear, but the child is forced to rely mostly on his visual system to follow and understand the information.

It is a well-known fact that TV presumes a short attention span on the part of its viewers. Most programs and especially the commercials, are presented as quickly changing flashes of situations, images, colors, voices, rhythms. This keeps the viewer watching. A child exposed to TV from a very early age, often for hours a day, becomes conditioned to the short attention span imposed on him. There is no need to sustain attention for longer than a few seconds at a time. But in the real world — at school in particular — situations don't change so rapidly. How can a "TV- trained" child be expected to pay attention for such a long period of time, without a cut, or a commercial break? How can he express an uninterrupted flow of ideas, tell a story or elaborate a thought, without being distracted by other thoughts flashing through his mind? My strong conviction is that many attentional deficit disorders are reinforced by watching too much TV.

Besides sounds, another vital source of energy for us is food. For highly sensitive children, including many with hyperactivity, the kind of energy they receive from food is critically important. Avoid food or beverages with high sugar content and chemical additives such as colorants or preservatives. While not particularly good in anyone's diet, they should be eliminated altogether from the diet of these children. A lot has been said and written about the effect of diet on hyperactivity.[2] Although it is certainly not the only factor at play in this complex condition, I know that a high sugar diet can definitely contribute to hyperactivity.

THE READING EAR

Decoding groups of letters at a very fast rate while making sense out of them requires a perfect knowledge and mastery of the sounds corresponding to those letters. But what about the child who does not have the workings of language completely under his belt before grade one? He may run into trouble as he tries to translate language into its written form, as he tries to read.

I will never tire of repeating how important listening is in language acquisition. And because reading is mostly a language skill, learning to read should be done through the ear — children should learn to read out loud.

Silent reading makes us forget the real purpose of reading. The French word for "reading" is *lecture*. "Lecture" in English now seems to have a different meaning, but does it really? Don't the expressions "giving a lecture" or "delivering a paper" mean reading material out loud? The original purpose of reading was to transmit written infor-mation to others aloud. It was long after the discovery of printing, when books became mass produced, that reading became an individual, silent activity, and the "aloud" component of the word "lecture" disappeared — in English as well as in French. When I try to explain to children what reading is, I tell them that one day someone had a story to tell. This story was so important and exciting that many others just had to know it. To pass the story on to more people than he could possibly meet, this person stored it in a box called a book.

> The original purpose of reading was to transmit written information to others aloud.

Reading means taking this story out of the box to tell it to ourselves and others. A book is not just black print-ed letters on white paper, it is a story that jumps out at us, like a jack-in-the-box. For children who say reading is hard work, I suggest a visit to a bookstore. If all those people spend all that money buying books, it is because reading is enjoyable.

Children with reading difficulties usually have two distinct voices: the one they use to talk and the one they use to read. The latter is not only scattered and hesitant, it is also lower in tone, poorer in timbre, more monoto-nous, and not as loud. These characteristics point to a voice with poor listening control. These children should be made aware of the difference between the two voices. A recording sample of both is a good way to show them this difference. Then, they can be asked to use the talking voice when reading. To their amazement their reading may improve instantly.

Reading out loud should not prevent the child from reading silently, but silent reading, which involves decoding as well as comprehension, will only be mas-tered once the "auditory reading" has been perfected. The Earobic Exercise 10 in Part III of the book will help use listening to its maximum effect for better reading.

THE WRITING EAR

Writing involves the same process as reading but the other way around. In writing, the sounds of language are rapidly translated into letters which have a mean-ing. In this context, the writing hand can be viewed as a "talking hand." It is used by the listening ear to write in the same way that the mouth is used to speak.

The primary function of the hands, fingers, arms and shoulders is to reach, hold and protect ourselves. The two levels of listening — the auditory and the body — use these parts of the body for a completely new and different skill: written expression.

The role of the ear in writing is particularly obvious

with children or adults who are able to draw well but have a hard time writing. This shows that handwriting is more than just drawing letters. Drawing is a purely visual-motor skill that does not involve the auditory, but handwriting does, because of the added language dimension — it is like "drawing with our ear."

If we had to be aware of every single sound we emit when we talk, we would constantly forget what we wanted to say. If we had to be aware of every single letter we wrote, we would also lose track of what we were writing about. Thoughts come in a flow that translates into a flow of sounds when we speak and a flow of letters when we write. Cursive writing is the most appropriate way to translate this flow. Printing, on the other hand, constantly interrupts the flow of thoughts, as it involves singling out every letter. Cursive writing is the best preparation for creative writing. Later, when the child has mastered the flow of writing, learning to type will be easy and fast. The movements of the fingers on the keyboard are like a dance of the hands that translates the flow of thought into language, as in the case of a pianist who translates his emotions into music. For both pianist and typist, the dance is choreographed by listening.

> If we had to be aware of every single sound we emit when we talk, we would constantly forget what we wanted to say. If we had to be aware of every single letter we wrote, we would also lose track of what we were writing about.

The movements involved in cursive writing can be prepared for in kindergarten by drawing and painting while listening to music, as I mentioned earlier in this chapter. The organized sounds of music induce organized body movements that facilitate learning how to write.

"Proof sounding" — that is, proofreading out loud — provides an excellent way of detecting errors in spelling and punctuation, omissions, redundancies, meaningless sentences, etc. The text can be read out loud twice — the first time keeping in mind the meaning, the second the spelling and punctuation. This practice of proofreading out loud is common among writers.

Teenage Listening

When I think of adolescence, what comes to mind first is a comic strip by Sempé, a French cartoonist whose work has often appeared on the cover of *The New Yorker* magazine. The strip is composed of a dozen images. The first shows a group of lads sipping drinks. They are stooping and look bored and apathetic. In the following series of drawings the same characters are seen racing in cars, making dangerous turns on a steep mountain road. The very last image is similar to the first: it depicts the same lads with the same posture, sipping another drink, except the place is different. Puberty and adolescence seem to be such jumps from extreme highs — high speed, high noises — to extreme lows — doing nothing, procrastinating.

The hormonal modifications that lead to the child's metamorphosis into adulthood make the teen years a time in life when the most radical changes occur. These affect both the physical and psychological fabric of the individual. The rapid changes of body and voice that start at puberty are the next challenges for listening.

It is not unusual to see teenagers grow ten to fifteen

centimeters in one year. Not only the body's size, but its whole structure goes through the transition from child into adult. At the time of this change the child's high-pitched voice also becomes lower.

More dramatic with boys than with girls, the changing voice affects the adolescent's level of energy. The clear, well-modulated and richly timbered voice of the child quickly becomes muffled, monotonous and lifeless. The youngster suddenly loses one of his main sources of energy at the very time when his rapidly developing body needs it most. Waking up in the morning becomes more difficult. The adolescent starts to resemble Sempé's characters: he becomes passive, apathetic and unmotivated. Boredom and lack of interest are two of the results of the energy loss. Those who grow tall usually have more problems related to the level of energy, posture and changing voice than others, since the changes they undergo are much more dramatic.

All these transitions of the body and voice take the youngster by surprise. The ear was used to one instrument, and now it suddenly has to deal with a larger and very different one. It takes time to adapt.

And so it will take time for a teenager to get used to his new body-instrument and to reattune his listening. The vestibular ear will have to re-attune to the new body and the auditory ear will have to adjust to this instrument's new sound — the adult voice.

This is only a phase, but parents and educators know only too well how long it can last. During this phase, the young person is most vulnerable to all the artificial means that will boost his energy and distract him from boredom, even if for a little while. Remember Sempé's characters racing along the mountain roads? Not only high speed rides, but drugs and alcohol can become these energy boosters. Strong sensory stimulations such as speeding or listening to loud music energize the

> It will take time for a teenager to get used to his new body-instrument and to reattune his listening.

brain and body. However, they often do so at the cost of damaging the ear or creating even more serious problems.

MUSIC THAT MAKES THE BODY ROCK

When I talk about music, my intention is not to judge it from either an aesthetic or moral point of view; my primary concern is the health of listening.

Is rock music — or any other type of music that youngsters like — "bad"? This is the question I am asked over and over again. My answer is that there is no such thing as bad music. What is bad, however, is the volume at which the youngsters usually listen to it. The music of Mozart would be just as harmful to the ears if it were heard at ninety to one hundred decibels or higher, except no one seems to enjoy listening to Mozart at such levels. But why does rock music have to be played so loudly?

Rock music is very rich in low frequency content. Low frequency sounds need more energy — more power — to be perceived than high frequency ones. Organ pipes for low-pitched notes are much larger than those for higher ones. Think of the difference in size between a double bass, a cello and a violin relative to their sound range. It takes a lot more to blow a note on a huge trombone than on a tiny flute. These are a few examples of how much more power is required to produce the low sounds. More power, more watts, translates into more volume, more decibels. To boost these lower frequencies, the teenagers increase the overall volume level, which makes the medium and high frequencies louder as well. That is why rock music tends to be played so loudly. The music of Mozart, which is rich in higher harmonics and has little low frequency content, needs minimum energy to be clearly audible. As a result, we don't feel like turning the volume up when we listen to it.

Another reason why the low frequencies have to

be heard louder is that they are not as energizing as the high frequencies. To use another metaphor, low sounds are filling all right, but have very little nutritive value. Turning up the volume is like eating more to get more energy, but more energy is needed for digestion as well.

But why are teenagers so attracted to low frequencies? The low frequency range carries the rhythm — a slow pulsation that makes the body move. Rock music is, therefore, literally the music that makes the body rock. Adolescents live in a body that is undergoing constant shift, readjustment, they are reattuning a body in constant need of strong stimulation. Rhythms provide the stimulation that is part of the teenager's process of self-discovery.

Music that makes the body rock is hardly a novelty; it exists in all cultures and has acquired a sacred or magical connotation in many civilizations. Rhythmic music allows the body to express emotional states such as joy, sadness, hope, faith — as in the case of African-American spirituals, which are the ancestors of jazz and today's rock music.

The body movements induced by highly rhythmic music allow the release of tension, leading to a sense of euphoria. Dancing is one way of releasing tension, but too much of it may drain the teenager physically and mentally. All of us at one time or another have found it hard to get up the next morning after a night of heavy dancing. When we have a "sound hangover," we feel groggy and apathetic.

The repetitiveness of rhythmic music tends to alter the state of consciousness, often putting the listener in a sort of trance. Some rhythmic music, prayer mills and incantations found in most religions are examples. Military music affects the body in yet another way. The rhythm of the drums is doubled by the repeated melodies played

> Rock music is, therefore, literally the music that makes the body rock. Adolescents live in a body that is undergoing constant shift, readjustment, they are reattuning a body in constant need of strong stimulation.

by wind instruments, instruments producing high frequency "charging" sounds. Military music induces certain body motions in a soldier, putting him in a state of euphoria and supplying him with the energy needed to march to the battlefield without giving much thought to the danger.

Closer to home and to the teenagers, rock music gives them a break from often intense, heavy and emotionally laden thoughts. The flip side of the coin, however, is that tunes continue to play over and over again in the mind. These obsessive inner tunes may act as listening parasites, affecting the ability to pay attention, concentrate or think creatively.

LISTENING LOSS

The main down side of rock music is not the music itself, it is the equipment required to play it. Rock'n'roll came about in the fifties and a great deal of the current music is a retake of this earlier style. But in the fifties, the sound systems used to play this kind of music were not nearly as powerful or as sophisticated as they are today. Back then, they consisted mainly of radios and record players.

The sound equipment that is available nowadays is far too powerful. We can all remember having our ears blasted and body shaken, passing by a "boom car." Not only the noise, but the vibration itself, can be felt from the sidewalk or from another car. Just imagine what those "boom car" drivers' ears and brain are going through, and what their state of concentration and vigilance must be like while driving.

> The human ear has a highly sophisticated protection system. However, it works only within the noise level limits of our natural environment.

The human ear has a highly sophisticated protection system. However, it works only within the noise level limits of our natural environment. Our organism is not adapted to the intensity levels created by modern technology and made available to the public without any prior warning of the possible dangers.

Generations of factory workers lost their hearing while exposed to a high level of noise. The only way of protecting them has been to reduce the noise level and to introduce ear protectors. The sad irony is that when huge amounts of money are spent to protect the ear against damaging noise on the job, even larger amounts are spent to find ways of increasing the volume of sound systems to please the public. Apart from excessive power, most of the cost of a sound system comes from trying to reproduce the most damaging sounds — the low frequency ones, which require gigantic boomers.

Until a few years ago, sound intensity to some extent, could be controlled by the environment. Usually one could not listen to music full blast because it was driving the other members of the family and the neighbors crazy. With the introduction of individual sound devices, music can be heard through headsets in places and situations where it could not be heard loudly before, such as in public transport, on the street, in waiting rooms, or at the gym. Because it does not bother anyone else, there is no more pressure on the listener to turn the volume down. The result is that the ears and the nervous system are exposed to horrendous intensities for much longer periods of time than ever before. And as if that were not enough, the proximity of the headset to the eardrums makes it much more difficult for the ears to protect themselves, thus increasing the risk of damage even further.

Exposure to loud noises provokes hearing loss and can lead to deafness. But long before it reaches such an extreme, listening is affected. We have observed that it takes days — sometimes a full week — for youngsters to recuperate from a "sound hangover" following a rock concert. In the meantime, attention span and concentration drop. The youngster is tired, passive, irritable and antagonistic. A full week of school may be lost and life may become unbearable for everybody else in the family.

"SOUND" ENVIRONMENT

I strongly believe that action should be taken to protect teenagers' ears. Excess intensity output warning signals or automatic volume controls should be built into every commercial sound equipment system. Noise levels should be regulated and routinely controlled in dance clubs and concert halls. At the time when we are trying to promote good health and respect for Mother Earth, controlling the sound environment of our youngsters is, in my opinion, important enough to be taken to the legislature.

> Exposure to loud noises provokes hearing loss and can lead to deafness. But long before it reaches such an extreme, listening is affected.

Unfortunately, to date little has been done in that respect. In the U.S., the number of state and local antinoise programs has dropped from 1,100 in the seventies to fifteen in the late eighties. In New York City, there are only twenty to thirty qualified inspectors to investigate thousands of noise complaints per year.[1] As a society, we have become more sophisticated in developing technology that creates generations of poor listeners and deaf youngsters. More than twenty million Americans are exposed to noise levels high enough to cause hearing loss on a daily basis.

We know that asking teenagers to turn the volume down is not enough. What, then, can be done to protect their ears?

MUSIC EDUCATION

Teenagers with a musical background — music students, for example — usually enjoy rock music as much as the next person, but they cannot stand it when it is too loud. In a group, they are the first to complain about excessive noise level and to do something about it. Loud music is not only disagreeable to them, it literally hurts their ears. Why? Because musical training is listening training. They have developed an ability to protect themselves against noises, an ability that is part of listening. When the sound level gets too loud, pain — a warning signal of the body — promptly reminds the listener that it is time to lower the volume or time to leave.

Musical education provides the youngster with a good protection system against loud noises. Preschool, as we saw, is the best time to start musical education and it should cover various musical genres, including classical music. From a listening perspective, because of the variety of instruments used, classical music offers the widest possible sound spectrum. Instruments such as violins and trumpets generate sounds which are extremely rich in high frequencies — the sounds with the greatest stimulating effect and the most efficient ones to train listening.

But often classical music is viewed as the music of older folk and the music of another class — the upperclass elite. Classical music is too often presented as a leftover of another time period. The clothing of the musicians of the orchestra, the language and manner of many radio or TV commentators or musicians themselves, reinforce the impression that classical music is a stiff art form, "for members only."

A more up-to-date presentation of classical music and its heroes can do a lot to raise children's and parents' interest. Even if some purists have good reasons to criticize the way Mozart was portrayed in *Amadeus*, such a movie goes a long way in making the music of Mozart more accessible. Recorded presentations of composers, such as *Beethoven is Living Upstairs*, let classical music into everyone's home. [2]

Parents are in the best position to raise children's interest in music. Most musicians are themselves children of musicians. When a teenager knows a variety of musical styles — classical as well as others — rock music becomes nothing more than just another style. It will possibly be the music he prefers for a time, but not the only one with which he is familiar, as is often the case. When trained to play and listen to music, the youngster will develop sufficient sensibility to respect his own ears, as well as those of others.

LISTEN!

In the early school days, "listen" may have meant work and effort. Now it means "accept the rules," "be reasonable," "obey." Adolescence is the time of life when the word "listen" may become deeply resented. I know many adults for whom the word "listening" implies authoritativeness — a leftover from their school and adolescent years.

Midway between childhood and adulthood, adolescents are in search of independence. It is part of the discovery of their ego, their self-identity. That is why the resentment of being told what to do, of obeying is normal at this stage. I am more worried about teenagers who are too obedient, rather than the rebellious ones. The obedience may well be a sign of immaturity, indicating an inability to make their own decisions. This indecisiveness makes them particularly vulnerable when facing the real world.

> When trained to play and listen to music, the youngster will develop sufficient sensibility to respect his own ears, as well as those of others.

How can we instill in adolescents respect for the rules and not resentment for them? How can we get them to listen without having to be told?

An adolescent finds himself at a crossroads; he is no longer a child and not yet an adult. The child in him still makes him believe in dreams — the dream of being an adult, in particular. With the impulsiveness of a child, he wants to act as an adult, have all the rights, possessions, and whatever else he interprets as being the privileges of adulthood.

When parents come to me with complaints about their teenager who may be skipping school, lying, stealing, or staying out late, I ask them first if their friends and relatives see the same things about him.

That often makes them realize that he behaves this way only at home, within the family.

I explain to the parents that their teenager is struggling to get rid of the child within and to try to be an adult. So everything that reminds him of his childhood is rejected. This process starts with the family and home. At home, the smells of the kitchen, the patterns of the wallpaper, the sound of the clock, the pictures, the tones of the voices are all loaded with memories of childhood and must be pushed away.

I then ask the parents what it feels like to go back to their own parents' home for a week or two. They usually say that at first, it is all wonderful — the smell of cookies, the old relics hidden at the bottom of the drawers, the after-dinner conversations.... Then, after a few days, they realize how difficult it is to make decisions in their usual way, to operate as the mature individuals that they are. They start relating to their parents the way they did when they were still living at home. All the experience and maturation that took place after they left home, mysteriously vanish. The atmosphere that was so relaxing, so welcoming at the outset, soon becomes suffocating. It was nice to go back to childhood for a short while, but then it is resented. It is time to leave.

I remind the parents that while they could leave their parents' home and go back to their adult life, their teenager still has a few more years at home. Therefore, something has to be changed. This does not mean changing the wallpaper, taking the pictures down or moving to another house — that would be too easy. It means the parents must change their attitude toward their teenager. They must forget the child and focus on the adult. Focusing on the adult means trusting the teenager.

Here are a few scenarios that I drew from my practice, where the parents' change of attitude has given the youngster an opportunity to listen without being told to. It gave the teens a chance to discover and to show a more positive and more mature side of themselves — their adult side.

• • •

Dennis's parents complained that he was absentminded, rather inconsistent and most disorganized. He did not comply with any of his home responsibilities. I met Dennis and asked him to choose a daily activity outside of home. He decided on a paper route. The first few days he had a lot of problems distributing the newspaper. Upset customers were phoning home because they did not receive their paper on time — or did not receive it at all. I asked the parents not to interfere. After all, it was Dennis's responsibility. He nearly lost his job, but a few weeks later, he was proud to let me know that everyone on the route was satisfied. It did not take long before he became one of the main characters of the entire block. The paper route had given him a role and an identity. The adult in him was able to come out. His parents commented on how much he had matured. Dennis was thirteen at the time.

Carol was fifteen when I met her. Her parents described her as a very difficult youngster. She would lie, steal, run away with boys, the list went on... In the small town where they lived she had the reputation of a delinquent. No parent wanted her as a friend for their own children. After a few days of treatment at The Listening Centre, we realized that she had a wonderful way of dealing with the younger children — the most disabled ones in particular. I asked the staff members to give her some responsibilities in the therapy room. She responded wonderfully — kids loved her. I told her parents what we had observed and asked them to let her babysit. They were most skeptical. With the reputation she had about town, how would she find anybody to accept her as a babysitter — could she even be trusted? I was so convinced that it would work, that I told her father that if one day she were to ask for a job at the Centre, we would not hesitate to hire her. He was stunned. Carol finally started babysitting and she did very well. The nights she babysat, she would do her homework to keep awake, something she would never do at home.

"Real" delinquents do exist, but there are not as many of them as may appear. When a youngster starts showing some signs of what could be interpreted as delinquent behaviour, I like to give him the benefit of the doubt — and plenty of responsibilities. It is, in my opinion, the only way to give him another chance.

Sometimes nothing done within the family manages to change the teenager's attitude. It seems that growing up at home is impossible. Not only the teenagers themselves, but the parents and siblings are affected. Home becomes hell. Is this situation a desperate one? It doesn't have to be. It simply means that the solution lies elsewhere, outside of home. Placement in a residential school or, if that is not possible, placement in another family — preferably in another town — are worth considering. It helped many teenagers, myself included, in their quest for adulthood.

As we saw, youngsters need to encounter situations that would draw from within themselves the desire and focus — the two ingredients of listening. Giving them responsibility, letting them find solutions on their own, will help develop this "built-in" inner listening.

Multiple Listening of the Adult

When Lloyd's manager told him that something drastic had to be done about his performance, he felt as if the rug had been pulled out from under him. He had been with the company for over twenty years, and identified with it completely. What was he to do now?

Lloyd had dropped out of school having failed several grades. After a few years of bohemian living, he had been faced with the necessity of having to make a living, and had joined this company at the very bottom of the ladder. He was a hard worker and got on well with the other workers. Slowly, his hard work paid off and he managed to climb to the top. But underneath the confident facade he had carefully crafted, Lloyd knew about the weak foundation of his skills. It had taken him years to feel relatively comfortable at work and to quash the insecurity that was eating him from within.

But his fragile comfort at work came with a price tag: his home life had to pick up the bill. He was mostly in a sombre mood, prone to depression, and became easily tired. Life with Lloyd was rather difficult. His wife knew better than to discuss his moodiness with him as it inevitably led to a big argument.

As a result of a recent shuffle, Lloyd had suddenly found himself in training for a new position. Having to re-adapt and acquire new knowledge at a fast pace was just too much, and the facade came crushing down. Lloyd knew he was making mistakes and could no longer compensate for them. He became defensive and abrupt with his colleagues and he was scared to death of losing his job. That is when I met Lloyd.

• • •

For youths, one of the nice things about adulthood is leaving school behind. But are learning difficulties really left in the past once school is over? When I assessed Lloyd, I found a listening problem at the root of his long-buried learning difficulty. Indeed, he never gave a second thought to dropping out of school, and nobody at that time attempted to find out why studying had been such a struggle for him. But the difficulty never left, and now, thirty years later, he had to confront his problems.

It would be naive to think reaching maturity means outgrowing all childhood problems. As we can see with Lloyd, a listening difficulty that went unnoticed in his childhood came to haunt him many years later. Lloyd's story illustrates how well an unresolved listening challenge can be temporarily patched up or compensated for and what the costs may be in the future. It also illustrates that it's never too late to confront these difficulties. (See the Listening Checklist, Appendix B to get an idea of what shape your listening is in.)

Regardless of your listening ability, it still needs to be maintained and to continue to develop, and for this to happen, it needs to be constantly stimulated. The many turns, many transitions, many new and unexpected events that come up in life all provide opportunities to use our listening.

For most of us, life unfolds as an uninterrupted series of changes, encounters, separations, moves, births and mournings. Energy is required to fuel the constant readjustments and reorientations. Sensory and mental flexibility and open-mindedness are needed to embrace the new horizons. Going back to school, learning to cohabit or to live alone again, changing jobs, developing a new social network, a new way of life, a new business — all these challenges call for the contribution of listening.

Adulthood takes different paths. The two most prominent ones are the personal and the professional, each with its own needs, obligations and priorities. Switching from one to another in a matter of minutes or seconds, as when a call from home interrupts you at work, is an everyday reality.

LISTENING AT HOME

Introducing a companion into our life and becoming part of someone else's life provide another challenge for listening.

Have you ever found yourself arguing with someone even if later you realize that you happen to agree with what he or she was saying? I know I have. You may agree, but you are reacting to something that irritates you about the person. Various things can put us off, and the voice in particular may act as a turn-on, as well as a powerful turn-off when it comes to communication. Voice, as you will see later, is one of the central tools and indicators of listening. Now, just imagine for one second what would happen if you had to live with a person with an annoying voice for the rest of your life — and that is exactly what often happens in a relationship. Two people can be very fond of each other, but if they are not on the same wavelength

— if their ears are not attuned in the same way — conversing may quickly turn into arguing. The relationship may suffer greatly for the wrong reasons.

To seek a solution, let's look at the people who are "forced" to share a life together. After all, when a monk decides to embrace religious life, he doesn't choose those he is going to share it with, whereas people in relationships do. Sacred chants play a prominent role in most Western and Eastern religions, and one of their possible purposes is to attune the ears and voice of a group of people in the same way — and thus to facilitate their communal life. Anyone who has ever heard monks in a monastery will have observed that they all have a similar quiet tone of voice and the same way of talking.

This is not to say that a couple living together should start speaking with the same kind of voice, but they should certainly both speak with a *good* quality voice. They should both open up their listening and make it work for them in their life together. The exercises of Part III are specifically designed for just such listening training and the voice exercises are an integral part of the Earobic routine. Why not do these exercises together with your partner?

PARENTING EARS

And then come the children!

Having a child is easy. Educating a child and providing him with what he needs is an entirely different story. And if his parents' listening is not available to him, he has two alternatives. He can either find a way to be heard, or not bother becoming a listener. In both cases the child will be affected, either by making life difficult for others — and this would be the "best" alternative for him — or by developing difficulties himself.

I mentioned before that the very first desire of the unborn child is to reach out, to communicate. This implies that parenting starts with pregnancy. The quiet dialogue between the mother and the unborn child becomes what soon after birth may sound more like a noisy monologue. Cries and screams suddenly invade the household day and night.

Hearing everything for hours at a time would be unbearable and listening comes to the parents' rescue in most unexpected ways. It gives them both an ability to block out the noise level, protecting their sanity. It gives the mother the opportunity not to be disturbed by the baby when he is just making noise and not to lose her vigilance when he is quiet. The mother is able to sleep despite the surrounding noises, and to wake up at the faintest babble of the child. This protection mechanism illustrates one of the most important functions of our listening. It is the silent role played by listening twenty-four hours a day, every day of our life. Ears don't sleep.

A lot has been said in previous chapters about the role of the parents at the different stages of their child's development. My experience with counselling is that parents most often accept advice and usually start implementing it with some success — and then they forget. What is most often missing is the consistency. Like many other things in life, there is always enough energy for the start. It then wears off and whatever was started is left unfinished.

Considering that it takes almost twenty years for a human being in our society to become an adult, parenting is a long term commitment. In twenty years the batteries may wear out more than once. Knowing that the more tired the parents, the more difficult the children are, energy loss can spiral and produce drastic results. It may leave the parents in a state of physical exhaustion and emotional disarray. It can erode the foundation of the couple's relationship and be at the base of a marital break-up. This is why everything should be done to maintain a high level of energy by keeping listening stimulated.

Counselors often advise exhausted couples to keep on talking to each other no matter what. Doing so not only keeps the dialogue open between them, but the sound of their voice may provide the much needed energy. This provides a constructive alternative to other modes of stimulation such as arguing and screaming at each other. Physical abuse, which is so common in families, can be an unfortunate consequence of exhaustion in relationships.

LISTENING AT WORK

Entering the workplace, with everything it implies, is also a new challenge. School and, for some, college, have been the centerpiece of daily activities for years. Now it is time to apply what we learned and to quickly realize that what we learned rarely works the way we learned it. We still have to learn but in an entirely different fashion. Learning has to be fast. It has to fit into real life situations. It has to translate into action right away. It involves our responsibility. This new way of learning is more difficult for those who have spent many years in the pure but rarefied atmosphere of a college, where the experience of life is modified, even distorted by the filters of campus culture. Life in the real world is quite different, and it is not unusual to see the most brilliant academic achievements not translated into a successful career.

Many people excel in their filed of expertise but still do not make it professionally because of their difficulty relating to others.

Listening must readjust into this new reality. A job interview, a meeting where one has to present and defend a project, a difference of opinion with a superior, are all part of a new world. One's "image" becomes extremely important. It is not just what, but how one says things that plays a role. Being hard working and motivated is no longer enough — one has to be self-confident and articulate, clear and concise in both thoughts and words. A new way to listen, to think, to speak and to act is now required.

Then there are the working relationships. How many people excel in their field of expertise but still do not make it professionally because of their difficulty relating to others? And how many people have years and years of their lives ruined by tensions, rivalries and petty arguments at work! The fact is that we usually don't choose who we spend our working days with. This forced cohabitation can be a source of problems. We saw how the monks solved this problem. It would be difficult, however, to ask employees of a company to sing Gregorian chant! What sounds more like a joke, in fact, exists in some countries such as Korea, Taiwan and Japan. Employees there sing the corporate hymn together. Some variations of this practice exist closer to home. Whether or not one agrees with such practice to increase production is another matter. The use of sound and listening to attune the ears of a group of people is not unique to those who live a communal life.

Work, be it physical or mental, consumes a great deal of energy, whereas the listening ear is an energy provider. The beauty of the system is that many jobs make extensive use of listening, and offer a wonderful way to get energized. Many people observe that not only do they work more efficiently, but they also feel better, more stimulated and on top of things by the end of the week than at the beginning. Of course, the excitement of the approaching weekend also helps. However, what happens after a "weekend's rest" is a lot more telling. The stories of the manufacture of poor quality products on Monday morning is legendary. Why? It may be that after a "good weekend's rest," the battery is flat and it takes the working week to charge it again.

The contribution of listening varies from job to job. Some occupations, such as nursing, waiting on tables, entertaining — acting and singing in particular — involve both levels of the ear because they combine social interaction and physical activity. While being in some of the most strenuous and energy-consuming types of work, those who practice these jobs benefit from the constant stimulation of the sounds they receive and produce, as well as from the motions their body is engaged in. Many opera singers are so wound up after a performance, they are unable to sleep that same night. The same happens with many actors and public speakers. Energy expended in this manner is clearly regained with interest, within limits, of course....

There are many jobs with a strong auditory component but with virtually no physical activity. This is the case with teachers, salespeople, counselors and most of the service professionals. Because of the lack of body movements, less energy is produced, but for the very same reason, less energy is spent. This usually balances out quite well. When listening and the voice are of good quality, one should feel and work better by the end of the day.

Those whose jobs have a minimal listening component such as accountants, laboratory technicians, draftspeople, translators and typists have less opportunity to keep themselves stimulated during the course of the working day. The situation worsens in the case of silent and static work in noisy environments — secretaries in large open pools or workers in factories, for example. The worst of all is when the walls, floors and ceilings are covered with sound-absorbing material in an attempt to reduce the noise level. These materials absorb most of the high frequency sounds and very little of the low frequencies. All the sounds with some "energizing" value disappear, leaving the person in a dead, muted atmosphere. Such an environment deprived of sensory stimulation creates tiredness, fatigue, grogginess and headaches.

If you are lucky enough to make extensive use of your voice at work, improve your voice quality and body posture to take full advantage of your situation. Make physical activities a part of your day, such as walks at lunch breaks, after work or both.

If your job is static and silent, physical activities are even more critical. But what you need most is to give your voice a chance to energize your ear. Think about singing in a choir or getting involved in community work. Reverberant material on the walls and mobile partitions in a soundproof space will make it easier for your listening. You will be surprised how much difference just a few glossy posters or pictures framed with glass can make. And why not have classical music in the background, especially if you are working in a noisy environment? For exercises to improve listening and voice, I again refer you to the Earobic Exercises.

> If you are lucky enough to make extensive use of your voice at work, improve your voice quality and body posture to take full advantage of your situation.

LISTENING RE-CREATION

As stimulating as work may be, the rest is well deserved, come weekend or vacation. But the challenge of rest is how to make it stimulating. This sounds easy and exciting. But why then doesn't it always happen this way? There are a few reasons. One is that for many, rest means doing nothing. Another is the implication of the latter: the less you do, the less you feel like doing anything; the more you think you are tired, the more you need a rest. And you know what happens on a Monday morning.

I agree with the saying that "a change is as good as a rest." Recreational activity literally means activity that recreates ourselves. My purpose here is not to provide a catalogue of all activities available for weekends and holidays. I just want to pinpoint some listening recreative activities that should be on everyone's priority list. They include: playing and listening to music, singing, dancing, socializing, playing sports and any other activity that involves both the auditory ear and the ear of the body.

Hunting, target shooting, loud music or anything else that exposes your ear to loud noises should be on your listening "What not to do" list. If your ears are plugged or if you feel pressure in your head after diving or scuba diving, add these activities to the list, as they directly affect the health of the ears.

Working without re-creation may lead to all sorts of critical situations. The two I describe here are closely linked with the loss of listening — one by excess, one by default.

"Too Much Is Too Much" Applies to Listening

In the inner circles of the listening training practitioners, we call a certain listening profile "the executive ear." The executive ear shows on the Listening Test as a drop in the higher frequency range. This drop is relatively common among people affected by noise trauma such as those in the military, hunters, factory workers or older opera singers. In the elderly, such a profile is generally attributed to the normal aging process, but it is most unusual among adults in their mid-thirties or forties who were never exposed to loud noise and have no family history of hearing loss. However, we have always been struck by the number of professionals in high pressure jobs who present this specific listening profile — hence the term "the executive ear." Sometimes they also suffer from disturbing ringing or buzzing in their ears. This is an affliction called Tinnitis; it is becoming more common but is still poorly understood. It is no coincidence

Too much is too much" also applies to listening, which can be affected by overwork and continuous pressure. Attention span starts to fluctuate, one becomes fidgety and distracted during meetings, mood swings are more drastic and decisions are made impulsively.

that Tinnitis is often related to high blood pressure associated with stress.

"Too much is too much" also applies to listening, which can be affected by overwork and continuous pressure. Attention span starts to fluctuate, one becomes fidgety and distracted during meetings, mood swings are more drastic and decisions are made impulsively. An extra cocktail becomes more and more welcome. Coffee consumption increases.

One's level of energy starts to drop, but one is too busy to pay attention to it. Workaholics stop listening to the warnings of their body and the environment. Their listening becomes too selective, narrow and rigid. Certain aspects of their life start to suffer. Usually it is their family. Then they begin to lose their friends and become increasingly isolated. Even work itself loses its attraction. They also become less efficient on the job. They may have a nervous breakdown or suffer from other depressive states. But life has endless resources and, with some help, they can recover. A good re-creative listening program would do wonders; then they may be able to resume a fulfilling life.

"ENOUGH IS NOT ENOUGH" FOR LISTENING

Once people feel that they have "done enough," they stop stimulating their listening. And their listening reciprocates by not providing them with energy. After all, the simple act of enjoying life and what it has to offer requires energy and drive. When you need to get your listening going — sometimes life itself unexpectedly gives the necessary boost of energy. Sometimes the best way to bounce back up is to hit bottom. There are many stories of people who make it to the top again after a war, a major breakdown precipitated by bankruptcy, depression, or illness.

I certainly do not wish bankruptcy or a war on anyone. I just would like people to realize that there are ladders in life other than those of a career, fame or prosperity.

OTHER DIMENSIONS

In my practice I often see people whose life seems to be just fine on the surface, and yet they are always searching for something that is missing. They may have started reading books or articles on philosophy, metaphysics or religion. As a result they may have developed an interest in the connections between the body, mind and spirit. Or they may have taken several workshops or seminars, experimented with their diet, tried out various meditation, or body awareness techniques, kept a dream journal, delved into their psyche, enrolled in martial arts or yoga. While they may have been fascinated by all this in the beginning, they still feel they have not found that elusive "something" they may have been searching for. It as if an opaque barrier separated them from that "other dimension" of life.

These people already have the motivation. What they need is the energy, the direction and the focus to help them with their search. And that is where listening comes in. It will help these people realize that this "other dimension" is not elsewhere, it is within them, and the Earobic Exercises offer a possible means of tapping this inner energy. This regained energy will help them to optimize the techniques that suit their needs.

Whether spiritual or material, a quest is still a quest. People who come to me in search of this "other dimension" are more alike than they might think. Far be it for me to dictate one or another direction in life — it is up to you to make that kind of choice, and stimulated and revived listening will help you to do so.

No Retirement for Listening

Retirement can and should be a wonderful experience. It is the time in life to restart the projects and activities that had to be put aside. These pastimes may include art, reading, studying, travelling, gardening and so on.

Unfortunately, retirement is often viewed as a long, extended rest, and rest too often means doing nothing. I have already said that the more we rest, the more we need to rest. Doing nothing doesn't recharge the battery. This is especially true for those who have had an active and fulfilling career and as a result have had no time or inclination to consider their retirement. For them retirement means having the time to play more golf, to travel more, to stay away from the city, to move to the sunbelt.... After all, can busy people imagine a life that is not packed with activities?

This sudden interruption of the daily routine takes people by surprise. It shows in the form of increased tiredness, which makes them feel they really need to rest; and so begins the vicious circle of self-induced depression that can accelerate the aging process. The vicious circle is reinforced by the well-rooted belief that "I am tired because I am old," which in reality should be understood as "because I make myself believe I am old, I make myself tired."

Retirement should be welcome. However, it should not be viewed as a dream that may come true one day, but rather as a reality that is never too early to prepare for.

Why should there be such a drastic shift from busy, active and full living to having a lot of free time? To ease the transition why not work part-time or not as intensely for a while before you actually retire? Use the remaining free time to either further develop your favorite hobby or to start an entirely new endeavor.

In the list of possible projects, it is preferable to choose those that "feed" the sensory system, the mind and the body. A creative pastime, such as painting, stimulates both your mind and the senses. Landscape painting or sketching, with its long walks in search of an ideal vista, makes it a more "complete" exercise when it comes to its energizing value.

An even better plan is to include an "auditory hobby" in the list. Playing the cello or a flute could be a trigger for joining an amateur orchestra or a brass band. I know a retired man who discovered his singing voice and joined a choir for the first time in his life. Another went back to acting after a forty-year "intermission." If such an idea is enticing, the Earobic Exercises will help with discovery or rediscovery of your voice.

Going back to studying can be most stimulating but is unfortunately dismissed by many who feel that age has eroded much of their memory, concentration and other learning skills. It is true that having been used so little for so many years, these skills have likely had a lot of time to "rust." However, one should not be too fast to jump to the conclusion that they are "gone forever." The reading aloud exercise not only gets rid of the "rust" but oils the whole mechanism. You'll be amazed to see it at work. (See Part III, Exercise 10).

Making oneself available to others through volunteer work, be it for the congregation, the town hall, community services, the hospital or any social group, may be a way to add a new meaning to life, now that making ends meet is no longer a priority.

Just imagine how many people and organizations in a community could benefit from the support, help and advice of someone who has been a lawyer, a chef, a gardener, a teacher, a mechanic, or whatever else, for most of their life. Such a unique wealth of expertise and knowledge is most precious and won't fade if it continues to be used. Students struggling with homework every day could benefit greatly from some help from a retired teacher. Having the luxury of being able to offer the services that they have had to sell all their life is for many an exhilarating experience, only to be compared with the experience of receiving their very first pay. Gratefulness from others is a reward in itself and makes it well worth the effort — particularly when the effort generates energy for oneself.

People who are forced to retire and who resent the whole idea because their careers kept them busy and satisfied have to be particularly careful of the way they approach this new part of their life. For them, dilettante activities are not fulfilling enough. They run the risk of not taking these seriously, of quickly being bored and abandoning them. For those action-hungry people, retirement should be viewed as a full-time job. Whatever they decide to undertake or pursue, they have to reach a high level of competence to maintain their interest.

Many wait for this time in life to write a book. Others help their children renovate a house, build a cottage, restore a vintage car that has been waiting in the back of a garage for so long.... There are also those who become opera afficionados, experts on precolumbian mythology, orchid growers or golf "semi-pros."

For those who feel this is the time in life to reflect and meditate, I recommend long walks, and listening to music that conveys this contemplative state of mind. I also suggest that they use their own voice. As we saw before, there is a reason why members of religious orders who lead a quiet life of prayer and contemplation make singing and chanting an integral part of their daily routine. The Earobic exercises help people start on that path.

THE AGING EAR

It is a fact that the aging process is usually associated with a loss of hearing in the high frequency range. The sensation of tiredness increases and is followed by the inclination to be less active. It is also a fact that elderly people who chose to pursue their careers well after the age of retirement are able to maintain an enviable energy and activity level. It is the case of some artists, performers, politicians and scientists. Among others, Marc Chagall, Arthur Rubenstein and Pablo Picasso were able to continue leading active lives past the age of ninety. I recently heard about a lady in Massachusetts who is completing her Ph.D. thesis in psychology at the age of ninety-two. These are exceptions, but we all know people who continue or have continued to be very active well over seventy. A key to their health and high level of energy is their ability to continue to stimulate their nervous system by keeping the body and mind working.

My extensive work with elderly people undergoing sound stimulation leads me to believe that reintroducing physical, mental and sensory activity can help slow down the progressive cycle of aging.

My extensive work with elderly people undergoing sound stimulation leads me to believe that reintroducing physical, mental and sensory activity can help slow down the progressive cycle of aging. Interest in art, walking, reading, writing, socializing, taking care of physical appearance and hygiene reappears once this kind of activity is begun. Better sleep and health, as well as a more optimistic outlook on life, are additional benefits.

I started helping Mrs. W. when her husband became very sick and saw her again soon after his death. She was 85 when I first met her. Aside from the loss of her spouse which affected her deeply, she was suffering from vertigo and lack of spatial orientation to such as extent that living on her own was becoming hazardous. Having been a school teacher and choral singer for most of her life, it was relatively easy to introduce singing and reading out-loud as everyday exercises. At first she found them tiresome. Soon it became easier and after some time she began to thoroughly enjoy them. People around her commented that they did not need to repeat themselves with her. She was also more cheerful, and more animated, and she started accepting invitations again. Mrs. W. regained most of her balance and sense of orientation. The sounds she produced not only stimulated her auditory ear but also her body. She lived until 90 the way she wanted to — in her home.

> Mrs. W. regained most of her balance and sense of orientation. The sounds she produced not only stimulated her auditory ear but also her body. She lived until 90 the way she wanted to — in her home.

• • •

First to be lit up and last to give up — "on" twenty-four hours a day, no matter what the circumstances — listening is our constant companion.

Listening contributes to our growth, to the development of harmonious communication with ourselves and the world around us. It helps us deal with the major events and transitions of our lives: birth, school, adolescence, relationships, parenting, career, retirement and growing old.

Invisible, silent and intangible, listening is no less important. It has to be felt, understood and appreciated for its true value. It is our responsibility as adults to do everything in our power to pass on this appreciation to our children — starting before they are born.

The Earobic Exercises of the final section of the book will give you the support necessary to discover or rediscover your listening. They will help make your listening come alive and will help you use it to "tune up" your body, mind and spirit as well as those of others.

Part III-Earobics

When I give lectures and presentations, the first question I am asked is, "Is there anything that I can do on my own to improve listening, without having to see a specialist?"

For years, in answer to this question I was giving suggestions on how to protect listening and prevent listening problems. In the last few years I have been sought out by health-care practitioners and teachers who want more concrete, "hands-on" information on listening — techniques they could personally benefit from and apply to their clients and students. This prompted me to develop "The Listening Experience" workshop.

When it comes to listening, speech and language, my own life presented a whole series of challenges. Until the age of eighteen I had the kind of voice no one cared to listen to — not even myself, as I later came to realize. Following therapy, I practiced the exercises recommended by Dr. Tomatis, particularly reading aloud. Among other things, these exercises were designed to help me improve my voice and give it some impact. To succeed both as a clinician and as a public speaker, my voice had to change drastically. I had months of daily listening and voice exercises before I gave my first public presentation when I was twenty-three.

Looking back over the last two decades, I realize that the evolution of my use of voice, speech and language went hand in hand with an increase in my level of energy. As a teenager, I was always tired. I could spend entire days doing absolutely nothing while my mind was running a hundred miles a minute. I always had grand plans that never saw the light of day. My energy was blocked. Now, with my busy schedule of long work days and no weekends, I often get little sleep for weeks at a time. The energy flow is not blocked anymore; it is there when I need it.

Many times I have observed the release of this energy flow with my clients. At the end of the therapy, they are asked to do listening and voice exercises at home. During follow-up interviews, clients do not have to tell me if they have kept up the exercises. Their voice quality and body posture speak for themselves. Listening reports to us directly if it has been well taken care of.

The Earobic Exercises presented here are drawn from the Listening Experience workshop and were inspired by the teachings of Dr. Tomatis.

To do earobics you will need:

- A cassette deck
- A recording of a violin concerto of Mozart
- A recording of the Caprices by Paganini
- A recording of a voice, be it singing or speaking, or a radio
- One or several texts (story or poetry)
- A hand mirror
- An adjustable high stool, preferably without a back
- a pre-recorded tape of progressively filtered music. (See order form)

EAROBICS 1: THE LISTENING POSTURE

Have you ever seen a rabbit in the meadow and what happens when it hears a slight noise? The rabbit's body instantly changes — it straightens up, its ears elongate and become erect. Alerted by the noise, the rabbit puts both the body and the auditory ear into a listening posture.

The way we use both our body and our ears to listen is quite similar to the rabbit's — only a bit more discreet. Listening starts with the body. This exercise is to help you learn how to use your body for maximum sound reception — maximum listening.

The listening posture exposes the parts of the body that have the most nerve endings — the palms of the hands, the soles of the feet, the inward sides of the arms and legs, the front of the body and the face. The position of the sitting Buddha and the "Lotus" position in yoga are two excellent examples of a good listening posture.

Before you begin, read all the instructions. Insert a Mozart violin concerto on your stereo at a comfortable volume and sit on a high stool.

Let's work on the body from bottom to top.

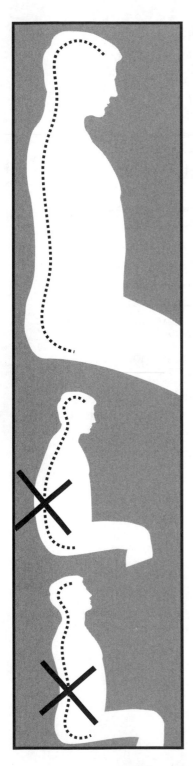

Legs

Adjust the stool to such a height that your knees are slightly lower than your hips. Sit on the front of the stool with feet apart, planted flat on the floor. Your knees are directly over your feet. Pressure should be felt over the arch of the foot through to the ball of the foot (in the back of the big toe); it should feel as if you're creating a base at this point of your foot. Sitting that way helps put the pelvis in a forward position to avoid arching the lower back. This also helps lower the diaphragm. One way to check if you are sitting correctly is that if you wanted to get up, you could do so easily.

Trunk

Your back should be straight, but not tight, with minimum muscle tension. To adjust it, push your pelvis forward, open up your shoulders and breathe slowly and deeply.

Picture your spine from the pelvis through the crown of the head, as though you are climbing a ladder. Each vertebra is a rung of the ladder. The head is the last rung.

Those who have a curved back should take particular care to open the shoulders. Rotating the arms backward will help. Stooping posture inhibits proper breathing and, as you will see later, voice production. You know your shoulders are open when you can draw a horizontal line on your clavicle bones.

Head

Lean your head slightly forward, chin down and close your eyes. You find the right angle between the neck and the head by gently nodding the head "yes", "yes", "yes."

Breathing

Deeper breathing involves an awareness of all the space available for the lungs as they expand. Imagine two air reservoirs. The first one — the lower reservoir — is located just above the diaphragm, under the ribs. The second one fills all the space behind the ribs.

Start the breathing cycle by inhaling and slowly filling reservoir one and two. Keep the air in for a few seconds, then exhale by emptying reservoir one then two.

To keep your back straight without muscular tension, use your arms and hands to support yourself. Don't hesitate to lean on them. Remember — it is your breathing not your muscles that should keep you straight.

Sitting in this posture, keep your eyes closed and enjoy the music for about ten minutes. This will be the posture used in all ten Earobic exercises.

When you sit this way, do you feel lighter? If so, it is because the body surface exposed to gravity is reduced. As a result, energy is saved and muscle tone is increased, making it easier to sustain the posture — you don't need a back support to sit straight. Now the two levels of the ear — body and auditory — are ready for listening.

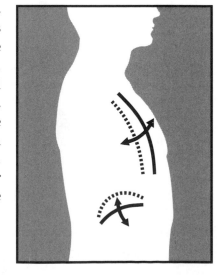

Earobics 2

This exercise was originally developed to be used with a special prerecorded tape I have devised for the Listening Experience workshop. (See order form at the back of the book.) If you do not have this tape, a regular recording of Mozart will do.

The tape is a 10 minute long recording of filtered music. It starts out with the normal sound of Mozart's music. The music then becomes progressively more filtered. By "filtered" I mean that the frequencies below a certain level are taken out, with only those above this level remaining. Thus, in the first part of the tape the filtration level increases from lower to higher frequencies. The end result is that nothing but the high harmonics of the music are left. In the second part of the tape, the filtered out frequencies are re-introduced one by one, until the "original Mozart" is restored on all frequency levels.

• • •

Start the tape and close your eyes. Assume the listening posture. Your body is now straight, but without tension. Breathe slowly and deeply, filling your chest with air from the bottom up. Your breathing maintains your posture without having to rely on the muscles. Your shoulders are open.

Your eyes closed, "picture" the music as if it were a mountain of sounds. The low sounds, those of the cellos, are at the bottom, with the high-pitched notes of the violin and the harmonics on top. Then, when you hear lower frequencies visualize yourself climbing towards the summit — the higher harmonics.

To help you with the climb, imagine a rope hanging from the ceiling and attached to the top of your head. Imagine that this rope is the extension of your spine, pulling you upwards. You physically feel that you are getting taller. Your body is becoming lighter; your ears, the muscles and the skin of your face are also being pulled towards the top of the head. Only your lips are projected forward, without any effort.

Like the rabbit, pulling your ears up and perceiving much beyond the higher notes of the violins, you are listening for the high harmonics, the overtones.

You might find it helpful to picture your face as one of an ancient Egyptian figure — an oblong shaped skull with the lips slightly pushed forward (see figure).

Continue to breathe slowly. The air goes in and out on its own. You feel light, you are calm and relaxed, you are filled with the music. You are listening to the high frequency sounds.

Now, be ready for the defiltering of the sound — the progressive reintroduction of the lower frequencies. Now listen in reverse — from high to low frequencies. Don't follow the sound as it comes down. When instruments with lower frequencies, such as the cello, are progressively reintroduced, try to keep your listening attuned to the high frequency sounds — particularly the high pitches of the violin. From this new "point of listening," you can enjoy a new dimension, a new texture of sound — it is a new listening experience of music. This is what listening should be and what, after some exercising, it will become. The key is to continue listening to the high frequency sounds, the energizing sounds.

• • •

Listening this way is especially helpful when conversing in a noisy environment. You can pick out the voice you want to listen to and focus on it ignoring the background, or low frequency sounds.

EAROBICS 3

Just as we have two hands and two eyes, we have two ears — two ears that look alike and, for most of us, hear the same way. The use of both our ears permits us to perceive "stereophonically".

When we perform voluntary acts, one side of our body becomes dominant. This is easily seen in the case of hands, but the same is true for the eyes and ears. When we look at something, one eye becomes dominant, just as when we listen, one ear takes the lead. For listening to be most efficient in verbal communication, the right ear should have the leading role, since it is the ear with the most neural connections to the left hemisphere of the brain — the so-called "language brain".

There are three steps in this exercise: Step 1 is to become aware of having two ears by making them operate independently, Step 2 is to utilize the right ear as the leading ear and Step 3 is to re-integrate the left ear into the listening process.

Language sounds will do best for this exercise. You can use recordings of poetry, story telling or even listen to the news on the radio. It is preferable to use a single sound source that you should face directly.

STEP 1

Take up the listening posture and listen for high frequency sounds (as in Earobics 1 and 2).

Sit still, close your eyes, and listen to the sounds. Now, "tell" your left ear to "catch" the high frequency sounds. When the sounds are clearly perceived on the left side, switch to the right. Now that you hear the sounds with the right ear, switch back to the left — then back again — and again. You may find it helpful to imagine a flexible hose linking the sound source with one ear first, then the other, etc. Do this for 2 or 3 minutes.

Step 2

Return to listening with your right ear. Now, very slowly, rotate the stool to the right exposing your left ear to the sound source while continuing to listen with the right ear. When you feel that your right ear is losing its lead, slowly rotate back until you "connect" and the right ear is dominant again. Rotate again so that you're increasingly exposing your left ear to the sound source but still leading with the right ear. With this exercise, you can actively and consciously control your listening and train your right ear to become dominant.

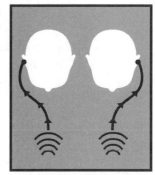

Continue to exercise your right ear in this way for the next five minutes.

Step 3

In the listening posture, face the sound source and listen with the right ear. Now slowly imagine your right car on the top of your head. To do this, imagine your ear is facing the sound source and is on the top of your head. You're listening with both ears but the right one remains dominant. Listen from the high frequency sounds to the low ones. You feel light and tall. Breathe slowly, effortlessly. Your eyes are closed and you stay in this posture for another five minutes. Listen with the right ear centered to the high frequency sounds.

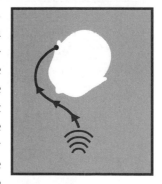

What you perceive as a centering of the right ear on the top of your head is actually a re-introduction of the left ear. You are now listening with both ears, using the right as the leading one.

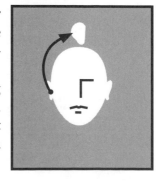

Earobics 4

By now you are comfortable with the listening posture, you know how to listen for high frequency sounds and how to use your leading ear. But you cannot apply this "new" listening to everyday life until your middle ear is exercised.

Listen to a selection of Paganini's Caprices, and try to imagine yourself performing these pieces. To do that, try to perceive each individual sound as if it were you playing it. Close your eyes, keep the listening posture, and continue listening for the high frequency sounds with the right ear positioned on the top of your head for about ten minutes.

• • •

The four Earobic exercises described above establish a base for good receptive listening. But we don't always have to rely on outside sounds to stimulate our listening — we can just as effectively learn to use our own voice. In the next exercises our focus will be on voice production from the point of view of listening, or "voicening".

VOICENING

When you decide to talk, your brain sends the message of your intention to the systems in the body that are responsible for voice production. The air propulsed from the lungs through the trachea hits the larynx, which starts vibrating and produces a sound. The vibration of the larynx is transmitted to the spinal column, which is located just behind it. This vibration is diffused throughout the body. The inner ear — surrounded by the bones of the skull — picks up this vibration by bone conduction and sends it to the brain. This is the first step in controlling the sound your voice is about to produce. It's the most direct and the fastest.

Apart from the skeleton, the sound vibration produced by the larynx is also projected towards the resonators — pharynx, nasal cavity, mouth and lips — before leaving the mouth as a sound. Once out, the sound reaches the ears via air conduction to once again be sent to the brain.

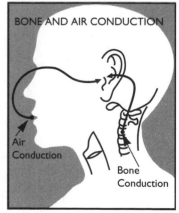

BONE AND AIR CONDUCTION

Air Conduction

Bone Conduction

The sound of your voice goes to the ears by these two routes — bone and air conduction — and reaches the ear at different times, thus allowing for two levels of control.

But what happens during the delay interval between the time bone- and air-conducted sounds reach the brain? The bone conducted sounds alert the brain to focus on a specific frequency range, which the radar of the middle ear targets. The same sounds transmitted by air conduction have to pass through this frequency channel that is imposed by the middle ear. The position, shape and tension of all organs, cavities and muscles involved in voice production — the diaphragm, lungs, larynx, pharynx, jaws, tongue, lips — are all controlled by the ear. The time that lapses before air conduction comes into play prepares the body in order to "fine tune" the articulation of forthcoming sounds. Tomatis has identified no less than 11 ear-brain-body loops that control the different elements of voice production — pitch, volume, tone, timbre, rate, inflexion...

Just keep talking and these multiple loops between ear, brain and body will automatically regulate all the sounds you emit. Considering that on average we produce 13 phonemes — or language sounds — per second, you can well appreciate the sophistication of such a mechanism. Voicening — the control of the voice through listening — works at such a rapid pace that it is virtually impossible to perceive or be aware of it when you are singing or talking.

Even though it is automatic now, this is the way we learned to use our body — to emit the sounds of our voice, and the sounds of language. If, however, flaws entered this learning process, they also became automatic and continued to affect our voice and speech. These "old habits" are so deeply rooted that we believe they are part of our way of talking, our "style." It may not even occur to us that something can be done to make things better.

Most likely, your voice can be improved even further. To be masterful and appear effortless in talking, you should become fully aware of your listening control — voicening. To do that, you'll have to dismantle your voice bit by bit to perceive, experience and analyze all its elements, and then put it all together again — "re-play" it — but without the flaws, leaving the "old habits" out. The following exercise will help you to retrain some important elements which constitute your voice.

For these exercises you need a high stool, a hand mirror and a poetry or story book. They are best done in a highly reverberant place — in your house it could be the kitchen or bathroom. Stairwells in apartment buildings have great acoustics, as do most churches and synagogues. Read all the instructions first.

Earobics 5

Bone conduction is the first step of voicening — this is where voice starts. And poor bone conduction leads to nasal, throaty sounds. The voice becomes hesitant, monotonous, repetitive, poorly articulated and expressionless. A singing voice may sound strained or

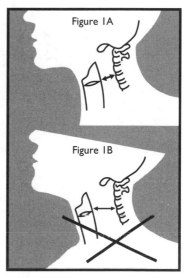

Figure 1A

Figure 1B

"ugly." Such a voice demands too much of the larynx, wearing it out as well as the speaker. These are the voices that annoy, aggravate and bore those who have to listen to them, if they haven't already fallen asleep.

Poor body posture is the number one cause of weak bone conduction. Therefore the first step in learning to produce bone conducted sounds is a proper voicening body posture. The voicening posture is nothing other than the listening posture applied to voice production.

To begin resume the listening posture.

Before emitting a sound, make sure your spine is perfectly straight. The vertebrae are all stacked one on top of the other, maximizing the transmission of sound vibration up and down the spine to the entire skeleton.

In this position the larynx and spine are as close as possible for the vibrations of the larynx to be easily transmitted through the bone structure of the whole body. (See figure 1A)

The position in figure 1B is to be avoided because it "blocks" the larynx, "breaks" the spine, and introduces a distance between the the spine and larynx.

Use the lower air reservoir — the one just above the diaphragm, under the ribs — for breathing. The upper reservoir remains filled with air all through the sound production. This helps to keep the thorax open without any muscular effort or strain to maintain the voicening posture.

Close your eyes, take a slow and deep breath and, while you exhale, emit a continuous sound. This sound is made with the mouth closed — it is a humming sound. Go slowly, softly, and enjoy this procedure, this delicate "touch" of the air flowing through the larynx, which is vibrating freely and without any tension or blockage. Feel the vibrations and listen to this transformation of air into sound. Emit a sound at the pitch of your choice, one with which you are comfortable. Throughout the exercise, change the pitch from time to time. This sound is soft and tranquil — nothing is forced. The larynx sets the pitch and the bones make the body vibrate — just as a string of a cello transmits the pitch to its wooden "body" to make music.

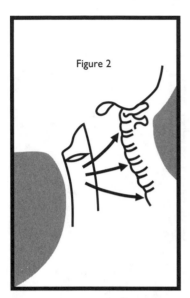

Figure 2

To ease this transmission of vibration, imagine that your mouth is at the back of your neck — as if you are humming to an audience behind you (See figure 2). We are so conditioned to speak to people in front of us that we tend to "push" the sounds forward using our phonatory system as a trumpet, thereby putting too much strain on the larynx.

Put your fingers close to your nose — you should hardly feel any warm air coming out. If you do, that means you are pushing the sounds out. You can hear the air mixed in with the sound, and the sound is harsh and dull. A good bone conducted sound requires so little air that you can hum for as long as 15 seconds in a single breath.

The bone conducted sound doesn't have any specific location in the body. You should hear the sound everywhere, behind, in front and around you. It is as if you are in a niche. At the same time, you feel a diffused vibration in the skull, neck and trunk — like a gentle massage that is very relaxing — a great way to calm down when you're under stress or to relieve headaches.

For the position of the head, remember the shape of an Egyptian statue — you feel your skull elongate, your ears continue to move up, your closed lips "fall" forward. You feel light; it's as if you are not making the sounds at all.

The tip of the tongue is touching the upper gum ridge — the region just above the gums. The entire top part of the tongue is against the roof of the mouth it literally fills up the mouth. (See figure 2).

Practice with tones of different pitch for about ten minutes. The higher the pitch, the taller you will feel. Try to avoid raising your chin, because if you do, you will push the sound forward again.

In case you still have difficulties making bone conducted humming sounds, put your hands with the fingers crossed at the back of your neck and apply gentle pressure. This pressure should not block the larynx, but should direct your head upward as if you were using your hands to pull yourself up to become taller. Feel the vibration in your hands.

This exercise can be done standing up and leaning against a wall, preferably a wall covered with reverberant material. Your entire spine, from hips to shoulders, should be against the wall, with legs stretched out at about a 20° angle.

Earobics 6

By now, you should be comfortable with your humming sounds. You can hum up and down within your voice range. Make sure that every note you emit is bone conducted — don't let it slide into the nose or the throat. The sounds of higher pitch may be tricky at the beginning. If you find that they are, don't force them. Rather, return to them later, when you are completely at ease with bone conduction within your range.

For this exercise, you will be humming a slow song of your choice. Let yourself improvise. Remember to keep your eyes and mouth closed and maintain the listening posture.

After a few minutes of humming, you realize that whatever you have chosen to sing has acquired its proper rhythm and its own beat, which is invariably the same. There is a slightly perceptible rocking to the beat of the song. This is the beat of your heart coming through in sound and movement — perceived by both ears — the ear of the body and the auditory. You are now listening to your heart sing. Your heartbeat and your slow, calm respiration give the rhythm to your song. So, physiologically speaking, this song is your very own.

By humming this way, you are rediscovering some ancient techniques of sacred chanting, such as Gregorian Chant.

EAROBICS 7

Now that you have mastered bone conducted sounds, the first step of voicening, let's move on the second step — air conduction.

Start humming, maintaining the listening posture. While humming, be aware of the sounds you emit — they have no specific location, no weight — and of the vibrations in your neck, trunk and skull. Your tongue is flat against the roof of the mouth.

As you keep on humming, open your mouth and shape an "o" with the lips forward. Your tongue hasn't moved. That means that even though your mouth is open, the pharynx is still closed.

Now let your tongue "fall down" in your mouth so a "g" as in "go" or "guitar" is emitted. Because your lips are shaped in an "o," "go" is what you hear through air conduction — or more precisely, a continuous "goooooo," lasting a few seconds. You perceive this "o" very much forward, as if it were projected out of the mouth.

While you emit the "gooo" sound, it's important to continue concentrating on listening to the bone conducted sound, to feel the vibration.

Put the tongue back against the palate, and close your mouth while still humming. If everything went well, the humming sound you hear now is the same as the one you heard before you first opened your mouth. To simplify, I have summarized the humming - vocalization - humming sequence in the following diagram.

```
                 hum                            hum
Inhale———————————Gooooooooooooo———————————————-------
close                 open               close
mouth                 mouth              mouth
```

Repeat a few more times. This time, continue with several short "go" sounds one after another "go.....go......go......go......".

With practice, you will hear your voice as if coming from two distinct sources — one is perceived as if it were behind and around you, and the other right in front of you. It sounds as if you were between two loud speakers. This distance, which creates the "stereophonic effect" of your voice, is due to the time delay between bone and air conduction.

The vivid image that comes to me when I practice this exercise — and even when I speak — is that the bone conducted sound of my voice is like music being played by an orchestra behind me. And the air conducted sound of my voice is like the soloist in front of me.

If you can't get the stereophonic effect I just described, it may be because your "g" is produced too far in the back of the mouth — too much in the throat. The "g" is the most posterior consonant of the English language; the more forward in the mouth you pronounce it, the more you move other consonants forward — putting the soloist even further toward the front.

The best way to learn how to pronounce a good forward "g" is to first produce some poor quality ones. This will allow you to listen and feel the difference between the two.

To emit a poor "g" take up a poor body posture for a moment (See figure page 158). Now say "g" a few times in either one of these positions. These "g" sounds come from deep down in the throat. They most probably sound raspy, dull, lifeless and tiresome for the larynx. Now, switch back to the good posture and pronounce a few "g"s again. You'll find it easier to project the lips forward and will have more spark. Be aware of the position of your tongue while you say "g".

Once you do the "o"s, practice other vowels in the same, continuous way: "gaaa.... gueee..... guuuu....giiii.." etc. Listen carefully to what each of them sounds like. With the help of a hand mirror, observe the way you pronounce them. The mouth should be open. Don't be shy to exaggerate this opening. The lips should be projected forward, even for vowels, such as "e", that are normally pronounced with the lips drawn back.

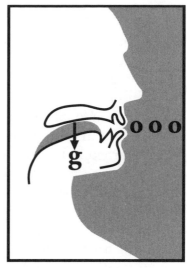

Now that you are comfortable with the vowels, you can chant the melody of your choice as you previously did with the humming sounds. While chanting, go from vowel to vowel and discover the numerous nuances and possibilities that the resonant cavities of your mouth and lips allow you to produce. You can also practice the voicening exercise while chanting the vowels. Start using consonants other than "g", keeping in mind, and ear, that they should all be placed more forward in the mouth than the good "g".

Continue this exercise for about 10 minutes maintaining the posture, the breathing and the awareness of the two distinct levels of voicening — bone and air conduction. Remember the orchestra and the soloist.

Earobics 8

There are two directions we could take at this point of the exercise program — voicening for either talking or singing. My clinical and personal experience having been more oriented towards language skills, I have chosen to talk about voicening in relation to speech.

This exercise is the application of what you learned in the previous exercises in relation to talking. If you do these exercises, you will develop more impactful and better quality speech.

In the listening position, hum, then chant some vowels for a few minutes — this is just a warm-up. Then start talking. Talk slowly, to allow your tongue, mouth and lips to articulate words. Imagine yourself as a sculptor using sounds to create words. Listen to the difference in your voice.

Continue to recite, count or talk for a few minutes keeping in mind, and in your listening, the position of the "good g". The very sounds you emit project your lips forward — if you are counting, spit out the numbers as if they were cherry pits. Exaggerate the pronunciation of the sibilant consonants — in other words, make the "s", "ch", "f", "z", "j" whistle more than they usually do.

When you project the sounds forward, your intention to give and share your message with your listeners is clear. But when you hardly move your lips and swallow the words, it seems as if you are not ready to "part" with what you are saying — you are sending your listeners a mixed message. Think about speech as a gift to others.

Earobics 9

Close your eyes and count aloud from 1 to 50 in the manner now familiar to you, spitting out the numbers one by one. You can exaggerate the "s"s and other sibilant sounds.

Now picture a short hose, leading from your mouth to the right ear. As you count like this, you will feel a sort of intimacy between the sounds of your voice and your right ear. When you reach this point, slowly imagine moving the right ear with the hose to the top of the head. You are now listening with both ears, and the right one remains the leading one. You are focusing your listening from the higher harmonics of your voice.

Keep counting. To facilitate voicening with the right ear, place your hand — specifically the junction between the thumb and index finger — about one inch away from the mouth. Use your right hand as if it were a microphone.

In fact, it is a sort of a microphone — and a very selective one. It picks up the high frequency content in your voice — those frequencies that are projected straight out of the mouth — and bounces them back to the right ear. Most left-handed people also benefit from this "microphone use" of the right hand.

Continue to count with your right hand about one inch away from your mouth. When your voice is connected with the right ear (remember the hose) slowly move the hand away — two, three, four inches, and so on — all the time continuing to listen to your voice with your right ear. Your voice should not lose any of its richness. When it becomes too difficult to hear these high frequency sounds, bring the hand in again. Feel how much easier it is to project the lips forward and to hear the sibilant

sounds when the hand is closer to the mouth. Continue this exercise for about five minutes.

• • •

Of course, you are not going to talk to people with your hand in front of your mouth for the rest of your life, but this is a method that allows you to more readily hear those high frequency sounds. The right hand is also a good speaking aid. Remember the link between the right side of the body and the left side of the brain, the language centre (See Chapter 3). An active right hand — thumb and index finger in particular — while you speak will keep the language centre of the brain alert.

This movement can be "camouflaged" by playing with any small object your hand can reach, such as a pen, a pencil or a letter opener... If you have to speak louder, get the left hand to follow the lead of the right one. I find this method extremely helpful in controlling speech flow and avoiding hesitations. This is particularly true when I talk in a language in which I am not completely fluent. When I have difficulty finding a word, I increase the movements of my right hand. Although this is now totally automatic, I used to have to remind myself to do it.

Earobics 10

I never tire of repeating what a difference the reading aloud exercise has made in my life.

Of all the Earobic exercises, this one is the most complete and the most efficient. It makes sense considering it is the culmination of all the previous exercises with the addition of the visual system. This is why it is preferable that you tackle it only after acquiring a good mastery of the other exercises.

Sit close to a table or a desk, take up the listening posture and breathe slowly. Remember that your lips are projected forward by the very sounds of your voice. Your right hand is like a microphone about one inch away from your mouth. To help support the hand in that position, rest your elbow on the table.

While reading, imagine yourself telling a story to a group of people — you have to grab their listening, captivate them. Forget that you are reading. If you struggle with reading, this is especially important. Your lack of confidence may be reflected in your voice, making it lose its impact, its strength and richness. You tend to mumble to yourself, and you end up with two voices — one you use for reading and one for talking — and your reading voice is poor in comparison with the talking one. A good reader has only one energetic and impactful voice.

It doesn't matter if you make mistakes, as long as you make them out loud, with a strong, clear voice. You have to listen to yourself make mistakes, to let your brain distinguish the difference between the sounds you emit and the letters you read — and trigger the correction. Don't hesitate to raise your voice when you come across a difficult word. If you mumble it — which is what is often done — you cut off voicing, making that word even more difficult to read — a common vicious circle among people with dyslexia.

The reading aloud exercise should be practiced 15 to 30 minutes a day — even more during exam periods, or when you are preparing for a public presentation.

• • •

I strongly suggest that you recommend the exercise to your children, or, if you are a teacher, to your students. It can make all the difference in the world for them.

If you recommend this exercise to students with reading and learning problems, I advise you not to "push" if they resist. More than just useless — that would be counter-productive and even harmful to their motivation. Resistance to the reading aloud exercise is one of the clearest indicators which I know of in identifying a listening problem. To overcome it might well require therapeutic intervention of the listening training program.

This exercise is most helpful when you are tired or depressed, when your brain is fogged and you feel like doing nothing, when you are bored and you have a hard time pulling yourself and your ideas together. Like humming (Earobics 5), reading aloud is an efficient way to reduce tension headaches. It makes you feel light, awake, vigilant, on top of things. It helps you to think clearly and to get your mind and ideas organized.

EAROBICS: FOLLOW-UP

I recommend you do the Earobics series twice a week for the first four weeks. Every session will take about an hour and a half. For the following two months, as you become more familiar with the exercises, you can reduce the time to thirty minutes.

After three months, the only daily earobics that will remain is the reading out loud exercise. It is the one exercise that consists of elements from all the other exercises. Reading out loud should be done for a minimum of fifteen minutes a day. If you are a student, try to read aloud for about thirty minutes a day for as long as your studies last. If your daily activity requires a lot of talking, reading out loud can be interrupted after six months. If it is not the case, it is to your benefit to continue.

Nothing prevents you from continuing to practice the other earobics, but your ultimate goal is to integrate them into your everyday life in order to keep yourself energized. There are simple ways of doing this. You may choose higher seats to allow for a better listening posture. When you are listening to music, select pieces rich in higher harmonics and set the treble knob or the equalizer to maximize the output in the high frequency range.

When you are speaking to people, try to place yourself in such a way that you listen to them mostly with your right ear. If you are face-to-face with the other person, you can both speak and listen with the right side so that you both end up at an advantage. You also can become used to moving your right hand to underline what you are saying. It will become automatic in no time.

Get used to listening from high frequency sounds down in any situation — at concerts, during meetings, listening to radio, watching TV. High frequency sounds are everywhere, even on the streets or in the subways. All you have to do is pick them out of the background noise and focus your listening on them. You will soon find that noisy surroundings are not nearly as annoying.

Singing or humming your favorite songs in the shower first thing in the morning can set the pace and tone of your day. It is an excellent way to get your listening and voice on the go — a shot of energy well worth a cup of coffee, and without all the caffeine! Singing and chanting can be good companions in your quiet and restful times, say, during weekends or vacations. You can even do the exercises while walking — this stimulates both the ear of the body and the auditory ear.

When communicating, we spend 55 percent of the time listening and 23 percent talking; the rest of the time is spent reading and writing. If you know how to listen and talk efficiently, you will be using your listening time to energize yourself and others.

Summary of Earobics

Earobic 1: The Listening Posture

Duration: 10 min.
Required: Mozart concerto recording, high stool.
1. Start the recording.
2. Sit on the stool with feet flat on the floor, back straight, shoulders open and head slightly forward.
3. Close your eyes.
4. Breathe deeply by filling in 1st, then 2nd reservoirs and exhale in the same sequence.

Earobic 2

Duration: 10 min.
Required: pre-recorded tape of violin concerto by Mozart, high stool.
1. Start the tape.
2. Assume the Listening Posture and close your eyes.
3. Listen for the high frequency sounds pushing the lower ones into the background.
4. Continue listening to the high frequency sounds.

Earobics 3

Duration: 12-15 min.
Required: any verbal language recording, high stool.
1. Start the tape and assume the Listening Posture.
2. Close your eyes, gradually listen for high frequency sounds (as in Earobics 1).
3. Listen to the sounds with the left ear, then switch to the right.
4. Repeat for 2-3 minutes.
5. Listen with the right ear, rotate stool to the right until sounds no longer perceived with right ear only, then rotate back.
6. Continue rotating to the right and back for 5 min.
7. Move the right ear to the top of the head and "plant" it there vertically.
8. Continue listening in this manner for another 5 min.

Earobics 4

Duration: 10 min.
Required: a recording of Paganini's Caprices, high stool.
1. Start the tape and assume the Listening Posture.
2. Close your eyes and listen to high frequency sounds (as in Earobics 1).
3. The right ear is centered on the top of the head (as in 2).
4. Continue listening for 10 minutes.

Earobics 5

Duration: 10 min.
Required: high stool.
1. Assume the Listening Posture and close your eyes.
2. Inhale and keep the upper reservoir full.
3. Exhale from the lower reservoir, emitting a continuous humming sound
4. Practice humming with tones of different pitch for 10 min.

Earobics 6

Duration: 10 min.
Required: a melody of your choice; high stool.
1. Assume the Voicening Posture and close your eyes.
2. Start humming the song.
3. Continue humming for 10 minutes.

Earobics 7

Duration: 10 min.
Required: high stool, hand mirror.
1. Assume the Listening Posture, close your eyes and start humming.
2. Open the mouth in the shape of an "o" and emit a "g" with lips projected forward.
3. Close the mouth and continue humming.
4. Repeat 6-8 times.
5. Practice opening your mouth with the lips shaped for other vowels.
6. Go on to chanting a melody of your choice in this manner.

EAROBICS 8

Duration: 10 min.

Required: high stool.

1. Assume the Listening Posture, close your eyes.
2. Start humming.
3. Go on to chanting the vowels.
4. Start to talk, count or recite slowly.
5. Emit "g" a few times.
6. Exaggerate the pronunciation of sibilant sounds while speaking.
7. Continue for 10 minutes.

EAROBICS 9

Duration: 5 min.

Required: high stool.

1. Assume the Listening Posture and close your eyes.
2. Count aloud from 1 to 50, "spitting out" the numbers and exaggerating the sibilant sounds.
3. Picture a hose between your mouth and the right ear.
4. Imagine the right ear is positioned on the top of the head, and listen from the high frequency sounds.
5. Put your hand one inch away from the mouth like a microphone.
6. Slowly move your hand away from the mouth until you can no longer listen to your voice with the right ear.
7. Bring your hand in again.
8. Repeat the exercise for another 5 min.

EAROBICS 10

Duration: 15 min.

Required: a text of your choice; table or desk; high stool.

1. Assume the Listening Posture.
2. Put the book at an angle of 90°.
3. Place your right hand in front of your mouth like a microphone, about one inch away.
4. The elbow can be rested on the table for support.
5. Start reading the text aloud raising your voice on difficult words.
6. Continue reading for 15 to 30 minutes.

EAROBICS: FOLLOW-UP

1. Practice the Earobics series for 90 min. twice a week
   for four weeks.
2. For the next two months, continue twice a week and
   progressively reduce to 30 min. a session.
3. Then, continue to practice daily Earobics 10 to 15 min., or
   30 min. if you are a student.
4. After 6 months, you may decide to pursue or interrupt
   Earobics 10 according to your situation and needs.

Long Live Listening

This journey into the world of listening has come to an end. I hope that, unlike the trips your travel agent books for you, this one does not end where it started, but like the journey of life itself, brings you to another place — another space — with its new perspectives. May these new perspectives enrich your mind, broaden your scope of knowledge, and elicit new thoughts and opinions. More importantly, may it enhance the way you perceive and deal with your own inner world and with the world around you, as well as harmonize the communication between the two. I hope this unveiling of some of the mysteries around listening gives you a new point of view — a "sensory" reframing — which will open new horizons.

If my "earcentrism" can be judged as excessive at times, it may be a reaction to what our society has done and still does to the ear — push it aside, assault it, if not destroy it altogether. It is logical that those who try to re-introduce the true dimension of the ear in our life tend to push the pendulum too far in the opposite direction. Part of my intention is to sound an alarm, to make others aware of the danger of overlooking listening. And I hope that time and basic common sense will put it back to the place it justly deserves.

When it comes to Dr. Tomatis' or my own explanations of the phenomena we observe, let me once again state that these are only hypotheses. A neuropsychologist familiar with Tomatis' work thinks that the "Tomatis theory" is not necessary to account for the results obtained with the Method. For her, other theories can account for these results. I am not in a position to argue. As I said in the beginning, I am a practitioner, not a theoretician. Tomatis himself often says and writes that, like many other theories, his is there to be challenged. What I can say is that Tomatis' explanatory framework greatly helps me understand my work, my clients, their difficulties and the changes we observe. From the practitioner's point of view, it makes sense and it helps.

While writing *When Listening Comes Alive*, my intention was to present the information in a "visual" rather than conceptual manner. This approach has helped me to interpret the world of listening and sound. I have tried to write the book that I would have liked to have read, when I was eager to learn about listening.

I would like this book to continue to evolve from one edition to another. To do so, I would most welcome your comments, suggestions or documents which could enhance future editions of the book. I hope to hear from you.

Keeping in mind Dr. Tomatis' much repeated saying that we read with our ear, I thank you for listening. Having read English written by a Frenchman, you may well have trained your "French ear" — an unsuspected benefit.

When Listening Comes Alive ... Long Live Listening.

Appendices

Appendix A
NORTH AMERICAN FACILITIES USING THE TOMATIS METHOD

CANADA
The Listening Centre
599 Markham St.
Toronto, Ontario M6G 2L7
Paul Madaule, L.Ps., Laura Lane, Laura Thomas, R.N.

C.A.L.L.
Centre for the Advancement of Listening and Language
408 Broad St., Suite 208
Regina, Saskatchewan S4R 1X3
Bob Roy, Ph.D., Blair Sirup

UNITED STATES
The Listening Centre
12800 Hillcrest Rd, Suite 101
Dallas, Texas 75230
Ursula Palmer Ph. D, Harl, Jimmy Asaff, Emilia Flores L.Ps.

Sound Listening:
A Center for Communication & Learning Skills
14674 S.W. Rainbow Dr.
Lake Oswego, Oregon 97035
Judith B. Belk, Ph.D.

Tomatis Center
2701 E. Camelback Rd., Suite 205
Phoenix, Arizona 85016
Billie M. Thompson, Ph.D.

Tomatis Center
55 Madison St., Suite 375
Denver, Colorado 80206
Ron B. Minson, M.D., Kate Minson

Listening and Learning Centre
135 Summer St.
Amherst, Massachusetts 01002
Elizabeth Verrill, M.A.

Tomatis Center
3706 Mount Diablo Blvd., Suite 300
Lafayette, California 94549
Pierre Sollier, M.A.

Tomatis Listening Center of Louisiana
3901 Houma Blvd., #109
Metairie, Louisiana 70006
Susan Andrews, Ph. D, Michelle Trumps, O.T.R.

The Spectrum Center
4715 Cordell Avenue
3rd Floor West
Bethesda, Maryland 20814
Valerie Dejean, O.T.R., Patricia Dixon, Ph. D.

MEXICO

Centro de Estimulacion Auditiva
Sierra Mojada 329
Lomas de Chapultepec
11000 Mexico D.F.
Psic. Gloria Assmar, Ma. Virginia Chenillo, Sra. Georgina
Moreno

Centro de Estimulacion Auditiva Sur
Chimalcoyotl #169
Colonia Torriellu Guerra, Tlalpan
Mexico DF
Ma. Virginia Chenillo, Sra. Alejandra Calderon

Centro Escucha Torreon
Guadalquivir 406
Colonia Navarro
Torreon, Coahila
Dra. Cristina Jimenez de Reza

Centro Tomatis del Sureste
Calle 23# 160 X 6Y8
Co 1. Garcia Gineres
Merida, Yucatan
Psic. Ma. Elena Muñoz de Lopez
Sra. Ma de Carmen Casares de Solis

Centro de Estimulacion Auditiva de Guadalajara
Calle Terranovas #1440
Col. Providencia, Guadalajara, Jalisco
Psic. Gloria Assmar, Sra. Maria Estavillo

Centro de Servicios Auditivos de Monterrey
Jose Benitez 2010
Colonia Ovispado
Monterrey, Nuevo Leon 64060
Psic. Refugio Reyes de Menchaca, Sra. Eva Santos de
Jimenez

PANAMA

Centro Auditivo Tomatis Panama
Avenida Cuba, Calle 4054
Buena Vista, Panama City
Sra. Eve Widnitzer, Sra. Rebecca Misrachi

Appendix B

A LISTENING CHECKLIST

We can not "see" listening; the only way to "get at it" is indirectly— through skills that are related to it in one way or another. This checklist offers a catalogue of such skills, and will enable you to assess yourself, your child or your students with respect to listening. There is no "score"; simply check as many boxes as you feel appropriate.

DEVELOPMENTAL HISTORY

This knowledge is extremely important in early identification and prevention of listening problems. It also sheds light on the possible causes.

__ a stressful pregnancy
__ difficult birth
__ adoption
__ early separation from the mother
__ delay in motor development
__ delay in language development
__ recurring ear infections

RECEPTIVE LISTENING

This is the listening that is directed outward. It keeps us attuned to the world around us, to what's going on at home, at work or in the classroom.

__ short attention span
__ distractibility
__ oversensitivity to sounds
__ misinterpretation of questions
__ confusion of similar-sounding words
__ frequent need for repetition
__ inability to follow sequential instructions

EXPRESSIVE LISTENING

This is the listening that is directed within. We use it to control our voice when we speak and sing.

__ flat and monotonous voice
__ hesitant speech
__ weak vocabulary
__ poor sentence structure

___ overuse of stereotyped expressions
___ inability to sing in tune
___ confusion or reversal of letters
___ poor reading comprehension
___ poor reading aloud
___ poor spelling

MOTOR SKILLS

The ear of the body, which controls balance, co-ordination and body image, also needs close attention.

___ poor posture
___ fidgety behaviour
___ clumsy, uncoordinated movements
___ poor sense of rhythm
___ messy handwriting
___ hard time with organization, structure
___ confusion of left and right
___ mixed dominance
___ poor sport skills

THE LEVEL OF ENERGY

The ear acts as a dynamo, providing us with the energy we need to survive and lead fulfilling lives.

___ difficulty getting up
___ tiredness at the end of the day
___ habit of procrastinating
___ hyperactivity
___ tendency toward depression
___ feeling overburdened with everyday tasks

BEHAVIOURAL AND SOCIAL ADJUSTMENT

A listening difficulty is often related to these:

___ low tolerance for frustration
___ poor self-confidence
___ poor self-image
___ shyness
___ difficulty making friends
___ tendency to withdraw, avoid others
___ irritability
___ immaturity
___ low motivation, no interest in school/work
___ negative attitude toward school/work

Notes

Chapter 2

1. "As the sound reaches the individual's ear, it is further modified by an electronic device Tomatis has called the "Electronic Ear" that presents the sounds in two rapidly alternating forms. In one form, the lower frequencies of the incoming sound are accentuated and the higher frequencies are diminished; this provokes a state of non-accommodation (passive hearing). In the second form, the higher frequencies of the incoming sound are accentuated and the lower frequencies are diminished; this provokes an accommodation or focusing response (listening)." From T. Gilmor "Overview of the Tomatis Method." In T. Gilmor, P. Madaule and B. Thompson, eds, About the Tomatis Method (Toronto: The Listening Centre Press, 1989), 27.

2. Testimonial of Dr. Klopfenstein (Head of Gynecology and Obstetrics Department at Hospital of the City of Vesoul, France) in Alfred Tomatis, Neuf Mois Au Paradis (Paris: Editions Ergo, 1989) 140-158.

3. A. Stehli, The Sound of a Miracle: A Child's Triumph Over Autism (New York: Doubleday, 1991).

4. Tim Gilmor and Paul Madaule "Opening Communication: A New Perspective on Autism." In T. Gilmor, P. Madaule and B. Thompson, eds, About the Tomatis Method, (Toronto: The Listening Centre Press, 1989), 95-104.

5. Wynand F. Du Plessis and Pieter Van Jaarsveld " Audio-psycho-phonology: a comparative outcome study on anxious primary school pupils, South African Journal of Psychology, 18(4) 1988: 144-151.

6. C.M.E. De Bruto, "Audio-psycho-phonology and mentally retarded children: an empirical investigation." Unpublished master's dissertation. Potchefstroom University (written in the Afrikaans language) 1983.

Pieter Van Jaarsveld and Wynand F. Du Plessis: "Audio-psycho-phonology at Potchefstroom: a review," South African Journal of Psychology, 18(4) 1988: 136-143.

7. Pieter Van Jaarsveld "Stuttering and the efficacy of the technique of Tomatis. Unpublished doctoral dissertation. Potchefstroorn University (written in the Afrikaans language) 1974.

Chapter 3

1. A. Tomatis, Vers l'Ecoute Humaine (Paris: Les Editions ESF, 1974) vol. 1 and 2.

2. For a detailed account of Dr. Tomatis's life and work, read his autobiography: The Conscious Ear (Station Hill Press 1991) Barrytown, NY.

3. R. Maduro, and M. Lallement and A., Tomatis, La Surdité Professionelle (Paris: Librarie Arnette, 1952).

4. M.R. Husson, M. Moulonguet, "Modifications Phonatoires d'Origine Auditive et Applications Physiologiques et Cliniques," Bulletin de l'Academie Nationale de Médecine/2 141 (1957): 19-20.

5. What I refer to here as the "auditory curve" is the so-called hearing threshold, or audiogram. This threshold is a measure of the mini-

um intensity at which a person perceives a pure tone at a given frequency level. The auditory curve emerges when the threshold points at several frequency levels are connected on a graph.

6. A doctoral dissertation in musicology by Gerhart Koornhof (still to be defended) demonstrates that there is a musical ear specific to the instrument the musicians play. For this study, Mr. Koornhof visited various orchestras and music schools, such as Julliard in New York and Curtis in Philadelphia, and tested the musicians' ears. He calculated statistically the typical way of hearing that corresponded to each musical instrument.

7. A. Tomatis, L'Oreille et le Langage (Paris: Editions du Seuil, 1963). A. Tomatis, Education et Dyslexie (Paris: Editions E.S.F., 1971). A. Tomatis, Les Troubles Scolaires (Paris: Ergo Press, 1988).

8. Although there is a general consensus on the involvement of the middle ear muscles in protecting the cochlea, it has not gone without challenge in recent years. The delay between the sudden onset of the sound and the protective action of the muscle would allow damage to the cochlea to take place. Also, the fact that sounds of dangerous intensity are extremely rare in nature, questions the assignment of such an exclusively protective role to these muscles.

For experimental evidence, see: S. Silman, The Acoustic Reflex, (Orlando, FL: Academic Press Inc., 1984).

F. Blair Simmons, "Perceptual Theories of Middle Ear Muscle Function," Annals of Otolaryngology, Rhinology, Laryngology (1964) 73: 724-739.

9. Erik Borg and S. Allen. Counter "The Middle Ear Muscles," Scientific American, August 1989, 74-80.

10. Additional evidence of this comes from observed heightened sensitivity to certain sounds (referred to as phonophobia), which is often one result of stirrup muscle paralysis. See: F. Blair, Simmons "Perceptual Theories of Middle Ear Muscle Function", Annals of Otolaryngology, Rhinology, Laryngology, 1964 73: p. 724, 739.

11. The middle ear muscles are active even during REM sleep, when muscle tone is completely lost throughout the body. See: E.R. Kandel, J.H. Schwartz, Principles of Neural Science (New York: Elsevier Science Publishing, 1985).

12. Erik Borg and S. Allen. Counter "The Middle Ear Muscles," Scientific American, August 1989, 74-80. F. Blair Simmons "Perceptual Theories of Middle Ear Muscle Function," Annals of Otolaryngology, Rhinology, Laryngology, (1964) 73: 724-739.

CHAPTER 4

1. A.Tomatis, L'Oreille et La Voix (Paris: Ergo Press, 1989).

2. J. de Quiros, "Diagnosis of Vestibular Disorders in the Learning Disabled" Journal of Learning Disabilities, 9:50-58 (1976). J. B. de Quiros and O. D. Shrager, "Postural System, Corporal Potentiality and Language." Foundations of Language Development (New York: Academic Press, 1975).

3. Jean Ayres, Sensory Integration and Learning Disorder (Los

Angeles: Western Psychological Services, 1992).

For a good overview of the roles and function of the vertibular system, refer to Jeff Robbins, "Vestibular Integration Man's Connection to the Earth", Somatics, (Autumn 1977) 27-36.

4. Harold N. Levinson, A Solution to the Riddle Dyslexia (Berlin, Springer-Verlag, 1980).

CHAPTER 5

1. A. Tomatis, The Conscious Ear, Barrytown, NY, Station Hill Press, 1991) 186.

2. R.M. Abrams, M.B. Hutchison, M.J. McTieranan and G.E. Merwin. "Effects of Cochlear Ablation on Local Cerebral Glucose Utilization in Fetal Sheep." American Journal of Obstetric Gynecology, 157:1438-1442. (1987).

In this experiment the structures of the cochlea in fetal sheep were physically removed. As compared with unoperated sheep there was a 75 per cent decrease in the energy reaching the brain through the auditory system. As the authors note, "virtually all grey and white matter were affected." These results imply that the normal growth and maturation of the brain depend on an intact auditory system, which is consistent with the findings of Tomatis.

3. Jean Ayres, "Sensory Integration and Learning Disorders" (Los Angeles: Western Psychological Services, 1972).

4. I heard this story numerous times from Dr. Tomatis, and it was also repeated by him in his interview with Tim Wilson in 1978. See: Tim Wilson, "A l'Ecoute de l'Univers: An Interview with Dr. A. Tomatis." In T. Gilmor, P. Madaule and B. Thompson, eds. About the Tomatis Method (Toronto: The Listening Centre Press, l989), 210-212.

5. We would recommend recordings of Gregorian chant from the Abbey of Saint-Pierre de Solesmes, particularly with Dom J. Gajard as the choirmaster. Chant Grégorien: Anthologie Grégrienne, from the Abbaye de St. Pierre de Solesmes. Dir. Dom J. Gajard O.S.B.; Accord Compact Discs 1983. Chant Grégorien: Noël, from the Abbaye de St. Pierre de Solesmes. Dir. Dom J. Gajard O.S.B.; Accord Compact Discs; l985. Gregorian Chant: Masses for Easter, from the Abbaye de St. Pierre de Solesmes. Dir. Dom J. Gajard O.S.B.; Peters PLE 031.

6. For more information on this theme, I will refer the reader to a very interesting study done by Brad Weeks sponsored by the U.S. National Fund for Medical Education and the University of Vermont, College of Medicine. This study assesses the therapeutical effects of Gregorian and Tibetan Chants. See: Brad Weeks, "The Therapeutic Effects of High-Frequency Audition and Its Role in Sacred Music" In T. Gilmor, P. Madaule and B. Thompson, eds. About the Tomatis Method (Toronto: The Listening Centre Press, l989), 159-189.

7. For more information on the importance of Mozart in the work of Tomatis, refer to A. Tomatis, Pourquoi Mozart? (Paris Fixot, 1991).

8. Marcia Davenport, Mozart (New York: Avon Books, 1979).

9. Paul Madaule, "Down's Syndrome: Just One of the Kids." An unpublished article (The Listening Centre, 1989).

CHAPTER 6

1. A. Tomatis, <u>The Conscious Ear</u> (Barrytown, N.Y.: Station Hill Press, 1991); 126-127.

2. Thomas Verny, <u>The Secret Life of the Unborn Child</u> (New York: Dell Publishing Company, 1981).

In addition to being an author, Tom Verny is also the founder of the bi-annual International Congress on Pre- and Peri-Natal Psychology and of the Pre- and Peri-Natal Psychology Journal. Both of these provide an invaluable forum for researchers and practitioners from around the world. Dr. Tomatis participated in the first conference that took place in Toronto in 1983, and his presentation is one of his very few works available in English. Among other works published in this journal is an article by Tim Gilmor.

See: A. Tomatis, "Ontogenesis of the Faculty of Listening." In T. Verny, ed. <u>Pre- and Peri-Natal Psychology: An Introduction</u> (New York: Human Sciences Dress, 1987).

Tim Gilmor, "The Tomatis Method and the Genesis Listening." In <u>Pre- and Peri-Natal Psychology Journal</u> 4 (Fall 1989): 9-26.

3. L.W. Sontag and R.F. Wallace "The Movement Response of the Human to Sound Stimuli," <u>Child Development</u>, 6 (1935): 253-258 J. Bernard and L.W. Sontag "Fetal Reactivity to Tonal Stimulation: A Preliminary Report." <u>Journal of Genetic Psychology</u> 70 (1947): 205-210.

4. H.M. Truby, "Prenatal and Neonatal Speech," <u>Pre-Speech and Infantile Speech Lexicon</u>, 1971 and in Word, 27 no. 1,2,3.

5. G.B. Elliott and K.A. "Some Pathological, Radiological and Clinical Implications of Precocious Development of the Human Ear," in <u>Laryngoscope</u>, 79(1964): 1160-171.

6. F. Faulkner, <u>Human Development</u> (Philadelphia: W.B. Saunders Publishing, 1966).

7. For a review of literature concerning fetal responses to sounds, see: A. Tomatis, <u>La Nuit Utérine</u>, 211-222.

8. A. Tomatis, <u>La Nuit Utérine</u>, 49. (Quote translated by the author).

9. A. Tomatis, <u>The Conscious Ear</u> (Barrytown, N.Y.: Station Hill Press, 1991); 130-131.

10 A. Tomatis, <u>La Nuit Utérine</u>, 53-54 (translated by author).

11. A. Tomatis, <u>Neuf Mois au Paradis</u>, Paris: Ergo Press, (1989), 159-178.

12. While the unborn child does not actually eat, his taste is already developed. "Perhaps the most surprising thing about this thoroughly surprising creature is his discriminating tastes. We do not usually think of the fetus as a gourmet. But he is one — of sorts. Add saccharin to his normally bland diet of amniotic fluid and his swallowing rate doubles. Add a foul-tasting, iodine-like oil called Lipidol and those rates not only drop sharply, but he also grimaces." Thomas Verny, <u>The Secret Life of the Unborn Child</u> 37-38.

Chapter 7

1. Thomas Verny, <u>The Secret Life of the Unborn Child</u> (New York: Dell Publishing, 1981), 22-23.

3.Thomas Verny, <u>The Secret Life of the Unborn Child</u>, 30-31.

4. Thomas Verny, <u>The Secret Life of the Unborn Child</u>, 21.

5. Frederick Leboyer, <u>Birth without Violence</u> (New York: Alfred A. Knopf, 1974).

Chapter 8

1. Marcelle Gerber, "The Psycho-Motor Development of African Children in the First Year and the Influence of Maternal Behavior," <u>Journal of Social Psychology</u> 47 (1958): 185-95.

2. W. Condon and L. Sandler, "Neonate Movement Is Synchronized with Adult Speech: Interactional Participation and Language Acquisition," <u>Science</u>, 11 January 1974, 99-101.

3. Laura E. Berk, "Private Speech: Learning Out Loud," <u>Psychology Today</u>, May 1986, 34-42.

4. Joseph C. Pearce, <u>The Magical Child</u> (New York: Bantam Books, 1980).

5. Marcia Davenport, <u>Mozart</u> (New York: Avon Books, 1979), 9.

6. A concerned parent may refer to a well-illustrated booklet distributed by Starkey Laboratories. This booklet, called <u>Myringotomy</u>, addresses not only how an ear infection gets started and develops, but also how to treat it surgically by tube insertion.

7. This figure is based on the survey of four hundred learning disabled students seen at The Listening Centre. Evidence to support this opinion can be found in J. Katz "The Effects of Conductive Hearing Loss on Auditory Function", <u>A.S.H.A.</u> Oct. 1978, 879-886.

Chapter 9

1. Teachers interested in knowing more about stimulating and developing motivation, listening and learning skills at school will enjoy reading the Rhythms of Learning. See: C. Brewer and D. Campbell, <u>Rhythms of Learning</u> (Tuscon, AZ. Zephyr Press, 1991).

Chapter 10

1. The clinical observation seems to be substantiated by a recent body of research which establish a statistically significant correlation between central auditory processing (CAPD) and attention deficit disorders (ADD). For a survey of this research, refer to: Donna Geffner and Jay Lucker, "Central Auditory Problems in Attention Deficit Disorders", <u>Advance for Speech-Language Pathologists & Audiologists</u>, Jan. 10, 1994, 5 and 42.

2. B. Feingold and H. Feingold, <u>The Feingold Cookbook for Hyperactive Children</u> (New York: Random House, 1979).

Chapter 11

1. M.W. Brown, "Research on Noise Disappears in the Din" <u>New York Times</u>, 6 March 1990.

2. Susan Hammond, <u>Beethoven Is Living Upstairs</u>. A & M Record Co. 1989

Index

About the Author

Born in France, Paul Madaule studied psychology at the Sorbonne while training with Dr. Alfred Tomatis. He then worked in several European countries and spent three years developing listening programs in South Africa. In 1978, Paul moved to Toronto, Canada, where he co-founded The Listening Centre. In the last 10 years, Paul participated in setting up Listening Centres in the United States, Mexico and Panama. In addition Paul has a busy schedule giving lectures and listening workshops. He is the co-author and co-editor of *About the Tomatis Method*. Paul Madaule is currently director of The Listening Centre in Toronto.

ORDER FORM

Some changes have occurred since the first edition of this book. The sound material to practice Earobics 2 is renamed **Earobics Series #2** and it now includes music material for Earobics 4 (Paganini Caprice).

A new double tape/CD named **Earobics Series #1** provides sound material and recorded instructions for Earobics 1, 5, 6, and 7 in the book.

Please send me (check the appropriate box):
Earobics Series #1: The Ear-Voice Connection
❐   2 Tapes $20.00 + $1.50 (Shipping) =   Total: $21.50
❐   2 CDs $40.00 + $2.25 (Shipping) =   Total: $42.25

Earobics Series #2: Exercise Listening with Music
❐   1 Tape $10.00 + $1.50 (Shipping) =   Total: $11.50
❐   1 CD $20.00 + $1.50 (Shipping) =   Total: $21.50

Earobics Series #1 & #2:
❐   Tape set $28.00 + $2.00 (Shipping) =   Total: $30.00
❐   CD set $55.00 + $2.50 (Shipping) =   Total: $57.50

Prices in US$, for Canadian prices add 50%

Payment enclosed:

Cash ❐   Money Order ❐   Cheque #_____

VISA _____ Exp._____

Name: _____

Address:_____

City_____ State/Prov_____ Zip_____

Send to: The Listening Centre, 599 Markham Street
          Toronto, Ontario, Canada, M6G 2L7

For more information visit **www.listeningcentre.com**